KT-498-733

The Buddha seated beneath the tree of enlightenment, from the pagoda at Doi Suthep, Chieng-mai, Thailand. Reproduced by courtesy of Soma Nimit Co. Ltd., Bankok.

THE BUDDHA

Michael Pye

Duckworth

First published in 1979 by
Gerald Duckworth & Co. Ltd
The Old Piano Factory
43 Gloucester Crescent, London NW1

First published in USA 1979 by
Duckworth
4951 Top Line Drive
Dallas, Texas 75247

ISBN 0 7156 1302 2

British Library Cataloguing in Publication Data

Pye, Michael
The Buddha.
1. Gautama Buddha – Biography
294.3'63 BQ882

ISBN 0-7156-1302-2

Printed in Great Britain by
Bristol Typesetting Co. Ltd
Barton Manor, St Philips, Bristol

Contents

Contents

PART THREE NIRVANA

PART FOUR MYTH

Preface

Our knowledge of the Buddha is suspended between little history and much myth. He was a man whose own personal experience was turned into a religion for millions. Our knowledge of the man is therefore indelibly marked by the religion of his followers. Usually the story has been told with miracles at the beginning and miracles at the end; though some writers have rationalised it entirely leaving little but a few dry doctrines. Neither of these approaches is acceptable from a modern, intercultural standpoint.

This book tries to take a completely new approach. First, in Part One, the bare historical facts are set out in their context. Secondly, in Parts Two and Three, the two great legends of the Buddha's Enlightenment and of his Nirvana are treated in detail. These were the two potent symbols of early Buddhism around which both the cult and the literature grew. These legends are like a corridor of mirrors, at the other end of which historical reality must be presumed to lie. Finally, in Part Three, the full-blown mythological version of the Buddha's life-story is given in summary form.

Buddhism is most easily understood through the story of its founder. The story has a historical form, a legendary form and a mythological form – yet there are certain threads of meaning which persist in all three, as the reader may detect. This is not a pious book; but the writer hopes that such threads of meaning are sufficiently apparent, and that these pages serve in some small way the critical appreciation of the Buddhist tradition.

M.P.

Note Names and religious terms are usually given in their Pali form, except in Chapter Two where the general historical context makes Sanskrit more natural. All diacritical marks have been omitted.

Illustrations within the book are taken from traditional Chinese woodblock prints illustrating the life of the Buddha.

PART ONE

HISTORY

I

The Buddha as History and Symbol

The man and the myth

One of the marks of a great religious leader is that in later times it becomes almost impossible to disentangle the man himself from the lives and minds of his followers. On this count the Buddha must be reckoned one of the most remarkable figures in the world's religious history. His statue has been raised in every Asian country from Afghanistan to Java and from Ceylon to Japan. In return the most diverse cultures have shared in forming the Buddha's image. On Indian stock have been grafted Grecian realism, Southeast Asian flamboyance and Japanese reticence. Over the centuries, one might guess, there is perhaps no other man of whom so many sculpted images have been made. Rows and rows of them stand in temples, others are scratched and chiselled in rocks and cliffs, more are painted on cave walls, silk cloths and sutra scrolls.

Quite apart from the impact of sculpture the traditional outline of the Buddha's life-story is also widely current in Asian countries. The story takes many forms, from the barest indication of the main points in the Buddha's life – birth, enlightenment, nirvana or decease – to volumes of such complexity that the general modern reader is quite impatient of following the thread. In these days of unprecedented travel and cultural interchange we do well to ask ourselves not only how the Buddha's story was told, but even more, what sort of a man this was who so imprinted himself upon half the world. For there was the man; and there was also, and is, the myth. Before attempting to come down to the bare bones of history, which however shall not be long delayed, it is as well to see some of the ways in which the Buddha was mythologised, and some of the difficulties faced by the historian. There are at least three ways in which the original man was transformed, by his devoted followers, into a figure who outstrips the ordinary way of looking at things.

The first of these was sheer story-telling. So many stories have been elaborated about his person that it is quite impossible to believe them all. Tales of the Buddha's life were still being spun centuries after he had died. Pious narrators told of his miraculous descent from the heavens by means of a virgin birth, of prodigious feats of intellect and physique by the young child, of trials of strength with Mara the king of the demons, miraculous escapes from death at the hand of his rival Devadatta, and of many supernatural deeds designed to convert people to the Buddhist way. This is hagiography: the writing up of a saintly life, exactly as it has been done all over the world in the history of our great religions. Very often it seems that the less resemblance there is to real life, the more the fantasies will appeal to religious credulity. Historical fact however belongs to a different mentality altogether.

The Buddha was also mythologised in cosmic terms. He was remembered not just as a saint in the sense of a religious hero, following a well-beaten track with special bravery and success. He was remembered also as a religious innovator, almost a saviour figure. He was the pioneer of a new 'way', and the founder of a new institution in which this 'way' could be pursued. Since this was believed to be the key to a successful resolution of life's problems, the appearance of the Buddha was very soon held to be part and parcel of the way in which the universe itself is arranged. To the Buddha himself, the new way originally had the character of a discovery, but to later followers the fact that he had once proclaimed it seemed to be part of the very world they knew. Thus the Buddha could scarcely be conceived of by them as an ordinary man who just happened to hit upon a particular method of self-realisation; he seemed rather to be the major identifier, almost the revealer, of the basic character of human existence. Since he himself was taken to represent in person the principle of enlightenment, it is perhaps not surprising that he was declared to be a 'great man' or indeed a 'superman'. For the same reason he was sculpted as a cosmic Buddha of huge proportions. He was even set in the context of an entirely mythological series of Buddhas who each in turn are said to have appeared within the suffering world. This illustrates the natural impulse of religious believers to declare that the key figure in their understanding of life is located at the heart of the meaning of the world. When Buddhists spoke of the Buddhas of the ten directions (eight compass points, plus the nadir and the zenith), it implied something like 'Buddha-hood is the stuff of the universe'. Eventually the number of reduplicated visible Buddhas based on the ideal of Buddhahood was taken to be 'innumerable'. But again, this is an expression of Buddhist understanding in cosmological terms, and it is not history.

There is one more line of imaginative elaboration which, unlike those mentioned already, has no parallel in western religious history. It is based on the fundamental idea that events follow each other through *karma.* For Buddhists this means that the factors making up each individual life have a continuing force which seeks issue in a further life, and so on for life after life, until they are altogether worked out. Each individual is followed, after his death, by another similar individual, who carries forward the burdens and fortunes of all the previous lives. It is only the perfected saint who can free himself from this endless recycling of life forces and attain nirvana 'without residue'. This implied to the Buddhists that until the Buddha himself achieved this state, in his final 'life', he too had passed through a countless number of previous births and deaths. During the course of these he developed various moral and spiritual qualities which gradually brought about the right conditions for his ultimate achievement. Stories about these previous lives, known as *jatakas,* were invented in large numbers, mainly to illustrate some point of Buddhist doctrine or morals. In the greater part of these the Buddha himself was presented as a king, or a monk; but he also appears as merchant, courtier, elephant driver, and so on, or even as an animal or bird. These stories are of some help in building up a picture of ancient India and of religious attitudes in the centuries following the founding of the Buddhist religion. However, for our knowledge of the Buddha himself, as a man, they are quite devoid of historical value. After all, a *jataka* story, by definition, does not even claim to be about the life of the Buddha in any ordinary historical sense.

Miracle and history

Western attempts to tell the story of the Buddha have had particular difficulty over the miraculous features in Buddhist legend, which of course the hard-headed historian cannot simply adopt. There are so many of these that the story, as a story, is bound to suffer from their removal. The great Belgian scholar of Buddhism, Etienne Lamotte, argued quite rightly that the mere removal of legend was not enough to establish factual reality. Moreover, he continued, if all miracle is withdrawn, nothing but a caricature would remain. One may agree with his verdict that writing the life of the Buddha is 'a desperate undertaking' (*Histoire du Bouddhisme Indien*, Louvain 1958, p. 16), On the other hand it does not seem right to follow his approach in simply retaining miscellaneous miraculous elements, abandoning our interest in what actually happened.

It is not only westerners who seek the simpler reality of the historical man. King Mongkut of Thailand, for example, who reigned in the mid-nineteenth century and was a fervent patron of Buddhism, chose not to have the story of the Buddha repeated in a style overlaid by miracle. Instead he promoted a simpler, more human version. Japanese scholars from the eighteenth century onwards also began to question the elaborations of tradition, and in modern times their contributions to historical research are second to none. Similarly there are very sophisticated monks in Ceylon today who admittedly may seek to maintain the traditional stories at a popular level, but whose own understanding of them is governed by a good sense of historical perspective. It is not so much a question of western rationalism versus eastern spirituality, as is sometimes supposed. The difficulties in sorting out and explaining the ancient texts are really the same in principle for everybody who is interested in them.

Even so, it must be admitted that the mythologisation of the Buddha's life is already far advanced in many ways within the extensive canonical scriptures of the Theravada Buddhists. These are the Buddhists of Ceylon, Burma, Thailand and Cambodia, whose sacred texts in the Pali language are the most coherent single early set of Buddhist writings still available to us. This mythologisation means that the seeker of historical 'biography' is forced farther and farther back into complicated textual studies, making use of parallel writings in Sanskrit and Chinese, hoping that some clear touchstone for dividing fact and legend will emerge. Alas no easy result has appeared. It seems sometimes that the more complicated the research is, the less probable are its results. Nevertheless certain broad outlines in the development of the Buddha's story are clear, and these will certainly be respected below.

Quite apart from the obvious features of mythology and miracle, there is one even more fundamental problem about the sources of information, which is usually overlooked. Patterns of narrative which seem to be of central importance, such as those containing the Buddha's teaching, are particularly closely tied to the interests of the early Buddhist community and hence are difficult to evaluate independently of those interests. More peripheral elements on the other hand, such as the Buddha's inconclusive encounter with a naked ascetic named Upaka, who refused to believe what the Buddha had to say, are so lightly treated in the text that we simply do not have a strong accumulation of historical evidence. The historian's head is threatened therefore with a double-edged sword. Either the information is determined by the concerns of the early Buddhist community, or it is of rather little significance. This means that the way in which the materials were important to the early Buddhists has to be kept in mind in any account of the Buddha's life. The context of their discipline and tradition is where the information available to us was crystallised and the original 'setting in life' is now more or less elusive. This does not mean, however, that the mentality of the early Buddhists is the *only* historical layer open to us. If their mentality is correctly located in the overall development of the legend, the first main growing points of the story do indeed have retrospective implications for the original events. This principle applies particularly to the story of the Buddha's enlightenment and the story of his decease.

'There is no continuous life of Buddha in the Scriptures,' wrote E. J. Thomas. This was the opening sentence of one of the most famous scholarly studies of the evidence for the life of the Buddha, now fifty years old (*The Life of Buddha as Legend and History*, London 1927, p. 7). Since he put such emphasis on the lack of an overall biography it is curious that Thomas's whole book followed the pattern of the much later works which do offer an almost continuous narrative. These traditional 'lives' of the Buddha, the *Mahavastu*, the *Lalitavistara*, and the *Buddhacarita*, which were compiled in Sanskrit, not to speak of the Pali work known as the *Nidanakatha*, seem to have haunted almost all western writers on the subject. However, to set out with a framework such as these writings provide, as so many modern writers have done, is really very misleading. It is rather like looking at Jesus of Nazareth through a mediaeval stained glass window. Even though the best writers have treated the legends with great care, or even outright scepticism, the impression has been created all too often that it was an outline of this sort, beginning with the Buddha's birth and infancy, which the first Buddhists remembered about the historical Buddha. Nothing could be farther from the truth. In reality certain *sorts* of things were prominent in the minds of the early Buddhists, and for good reason. These are his personal achievement, his teaching, encounters with various persons, his rule of life, and his decease. It is these which should form the main thrust of any modern account of the man. The elaborated biographies, although constructed partly out of these elements, came centuries later.

While this perspective on the historical Buddha is believed to be fundamentally correct, there is of course room for endless argument about the details. In particular there is still a great need for detailed research along 'form-critical' lines, that is, taking into account the literary forms and the changing perspectives of the early Buddhist community. Such work cannot be entered into here. Nevertheless a simple yet fair perspective on the whole matter can be stated in three categories.

i) The bare bones of history, treated in the next chapter below. This amounts to a drastically brief account of who the Buddha was, where and when he lived, and what any healthily incredulous person may reasonably take to have been the sum of his work.
ii) There are two key points of early tradition about the Buddha. These are the narratives of his enlightenment and first teaching, and the narrative of his last days and death.

These narratives are treated in Parts Two and Three of the book. They already contain a considerable admixture of legendary heightening. Yet their very existence shows that the main events were of great importance in the beginnings of Buddhism. While we should recognise here that we are looking into a corridor of slanted mirrors, we are nevertheless able to perceive some historical probabilities.

iii) Finally we come to the developed story of the Buddha. The various extended narrative accounts of the Buddha's life story are not all identical by any means. Their one common feature is that in so far as they go beyond the earlier sources they are almost entirely devoid of historical value as evidence for the Buddha himself. Nevertheless a collated review of the main features of these narratives, making up Part Four of this book, will show how the story came to live for centuries in Buddhist countries. Many of the early and fundamental themes continued to live on at this fully mythologised level, which thus itself became a vehicle for their communication.

In this way the reader can follow up the story of the Buddha's life, with a sense of reality, and without too many ifs and buts. Above all we shall not be swung continuously from stupendous miracle to humble fact and back again. The first three parts of the book show what a lot of reasonably 'hard' history can be told, without recourse to pious but implausible inventions. When we have arrived at a proper perspective on the Buddha as a man, in history, there is no reason why we should not also enjoy the myth. The fourth part of the book is therefore a summary guide to the elaborated but non-historical life story which eventually passed into general use.

2

The Bare Bones of History

When and where did the Buddha live?

Some people have doubted whether the Buddha ever existed at all. Although this is one of the highest forms of praise that can be afforded to a historical figure, the matter can be closed with the speed which it deserves. It is simply not possible to explain the origin of early Buddhism in a sensible way unless a creative leader such as the Buddha is presumed to have lived. This argument does not prove the reality of any of the particular details in his history, but it does enable us to point with some confidence to the time, the place and the character of his activity.

First however the names by which the man is known should be clarified. The most common are given in the following table.

Pali form	*Sanskrit, if different*	*Meaning and use*
Gotama	Gautama	A clan name, designating persons presumed descended from a common ancestor.
Sakyamuni	Shakyamuni	This title contains the name of the Sakya people to whom the Buddha belonged, and it means 'sage of the Sakyas'.
Siddhattha	Siddhartha	According to late sources this was a personal name given to the Buddha by his father; meaning 'aim-accomplished'.
Bodhisatta	Bodhisattva	'Enlightenment-being', that is, someone on the path of enlightenment; used for

	many different people in Mahayana Buddhist writings, but in Theravada writings refers mainly to the Buddha himself during the time before he achieved enlightment.
Buddha	'The Awakened' or 'The Enlightened'.
Bhagava	'Lord', an honorific title for a saviour or deity.
Tathagata	'Thus gone', a rather mysterious title suggesting sovereign freedom over one's personal destiny; in practice it is a synonym for 'Buddha'.

The ancient texts use all these names at various times, which readers often find confusing. Here the title 'the Buddha' is freely used. For one thing it is well known and convenient. For another thing it shows courtesy towards the man himself and to those who follow him today. It would also be quite satisfactory to refer to the Buddha by his clan name, Gautama (or in Pali, Gotama), and this is sometimes done below to stress his historical character or when speaking of his pre-enlightenment experience. The title Sakyamuni retrospectively associates the Buddha with the Sakya people, who were based on the city of Kapilavastu (or Kapilavatthu) in north-east India. It is striking that there is no historically well attested personal given name. Behind the impressive array of titles is a rather mysterious individual who grew up long ago in India. If we are historically sober we have to admit that we have no idea what he was originally called by his family and his friends.

It is usual to fix the dates of the Buddha's life by their relation to the much later accession of King Asoka (pronounced Ashoka) to the throne of the kingdom of Maghada in 268 BC. King Asoka belonged to the Maurya dynasty. His grandfather, Chandragupta, is the first king who can be located in the chronology of general history, by his relations with the Greek Seleucid dynasty. Chandragupta won a military campaign against Seleucus Nikator, gaining territory on the river Indus in the north west of the Indian subcontinent. Peaceful exchanges also took place. This ancient contact between Greek and Indian civilisations should not be considered a matter of surprise. After all, they both shared a common ancestry of language and of mythology. Indian (Vedic), Persian and Greek polytheism all belong to the same family. The grandson, Asoka, also exchanged missions with rulers of the Hellenistic world such as Antiochus II of Syria (reigned 260–246 BC) and Ptolemy III of Egypt (285–247 BC).

The main tradition of the Ceylonese Buddhists places the death of the Buddha at 218 years before the accession of King Asoka, that is, 486 BC. However, this calculation includes the remarkably round figure of one hundred years between the first council of Buddhist disciples and the second. The first of these councils is really legendary; and the second, although historical in character, is also without any evidence other than the Buddhist traditions themselves. Moreover the one hundred years in question disappear and resurface in a most mysterious way, and so if all the relevant texts are taken into account, they cannot really be reckoned as more than a symbolic statement of the passage of time. The main tradition also presumes that the Buddha lived to the age of eighty. This is based on a statement in verse given in the sutra on the Buddha's last days, where he is presented as saying that he renounced the world at the age of twenty-nine and had since been a wanderer for fifty-one years. These verses have legendary value only however; and eighty also seems to be a remarkably round figure, such as a creative monk might easily have taken to need a little more explanation.

It is these figures which give a birth date of 566 BC; 80 years before his death, 100 years before the second council, 118 years before the accession of King Asoka. Compared with the evident generality of such figures, the difference between 486 and 483, which is the main alternative date sometimes calculated for the Buddha's death, pales into insignificance. They have the same relation to history as so many crossword puzzles. The approximate picture is confirmed however in that the Buddha is always presumed to have been a contemporary of the Magadha Kings Bimbisara (reigned 546–494) and Ajatasatru (reigned 494–461), of whom Chandragupta and Asoka were the eventual if indirect successors. This means that the traditional dates are about right, though not to be taken as necessarily exact.

The position is illustrated in the following chronological table.

Accession dates of the kings of Magadha (read downwards)	*Ceylonese Buddhist Tradition* (read upwards)
546 Bimbisara	Birth of the Buddha (566?)
494 Ajatasatru	↑ 80 years
461 Various successors of above	Death of Buddha (486?)
	↑ 100 years
	Second Council (386?)
321 Chandragupta (Maurya Dynasty)	↑ 118 years
297 Bindusara	Asoka's accession (268)
268 Asoka's accession	

At the time of the Buddha the main torso of India, leaving apart the southern peninsula, was covered by sixteen 'great countries'. These were all regions where the Aryan incursors from the north-west had gradually, over some hundreds of years, obtained the upper hand. Still this did not mean a unified state. The various tribes and petty kings strove with each other and tried to settle their problems by the sword, by gold, by cunning and by marriages. Four of the most important kingdoms were Avanti, Vatsa, Kosala and Magadha, and it is in the area mainly dominated by the last two that the Buddha was active. This is quite evident from the great number of textual allusions to persons and places of the region. By contrast, it is entirely improbable that the Buddha ever visited the island of Ceylon, which is well over a thousand miles to the south as the crow flies, (even though he is supposed to have travelled through the air).

The area was that of the Ganges valley, lying between the bleak Himalayas to the north-east and the hills and plateaus of central India to the south and south-west. The great Ganges river itself is fed by a string of important tributaries bringing down water drawn ultimately from the snow-covered mountains of Nepal. The city of Kapilavastu, in the lower foothills, was the centre of the Sakya people with whom the Buddha is tenuously, but uncontroversially associated. The Sakyas were a minor republican tribe like several others of the region. A republican system of government by councils was also followed by peoples such as the Mallas and the Vrijjis, but these were also important enough to figure among the sixteen major states in the traditional lists. The later stories of the Buddha's birth and youth place him as prince and heir in a monarchical setting but this was undoubtedly elaborated to dramatise his abandonment of secular life. Nevertheless it is reasonable to accept that the Buddha was born into the Sakya tribe and that his life was mainly spent in the forests and townships of the neighbouring Gangetic states. The Sakyas were defined as a 'warrior' tribe as far as caste was concerned, and presumably they were in a state of progressive assimilation to the Aryan culture of those dominating the continent. How far this process had gone is a question which cannot now be answered.

Although the main Hindu castes were certainly recognised over the whole area, the intellectual and religious influence of the Brahman or priestly caste is thought to have been uneven. In particular, we should not simply assume that the Brahmanism of the eastern regions consisted straightforwardly of orthodox Vedic and Upanishadic Hinduism as we might now conceive of it. This means that one might think of both the Jain religion and the Buddhist religion as developments complementary to the spiritual philosophy of the *Upanishads.* All arose on the basis of a more or less commonly shared practice of yoga, whose origins are now lost in the mists of Indian history.

The Buddha's personal path

Whatever his original circumstances it is certain that the Buddha in early manhood abandoned the world of pleasure and power which able men of those times could either build, seize or inherit, and went off to live in the forest. He was, in effect, a 'drop-out'. We do not know what was in his mind, except in so far as his later teaching suggests it. Readers who are anxiously looking out for the story of an encounter with an old man, a sick man, a corpse, and a begging ascetic, will have to wait till later. There was a deep dissatisfaction with the ordinary possibilities and pleasures of life, which would after all turn out to be evanescent in the long run. Moreover there was enough indication of disease and pain and hardship to give the young man pause to wonder. This belongs to man's perennial questioning of his existence. Since the experience is widely known, but in this case without any really specific historical evidence, we may just as well quote some simple lines by the modern English poet A. E. Housman by way of illustration.

Could man be drunk forever
with liquor, love, or fights,
Lief should I rouse at morning
and lief lie down of nights.

But men at whiles are sober
and think by fits and starts,
And if they think, they fasten
their hands upon their hearts.
(*Collected Poems* 1939)

Most men think by such fits and starts that the problem quickly passes by in a new round of liquor, love and fights. But the Buddha certainly formed the resolve to abandon 'the household life' and to seek companions who could help him to find a deeper solution. The subsequent events will be explored in more detail below, for they belong to one of the two key growing points of the story of Buddha's life. Suffice it to say here that he learned the practice of yoga and got used to attaining trance-like states of mind. Since these abilities did not seem to have any effect on the fundamental problem of existence, he abandoned them to spend several years performing severe austerities. It seems likely enough that he did this in company of others, and that there were companions to whom he later returned.

Yet the answer to the problem of suffering existence did not seem to lie in the practices of fasting and physical hardship, in themselves, and so the Buddha eventually abandoned these too and struck out on his own as a solitary hermit. Even though he abandoned asceticism as a principle, the effects of years of self-discipline should not be forgotten. He was undoubtedly physically taut and emaciated, mentally and psychologically sharp, clear and refined in purpose. Various avenues had been tried and found wanting. Now he would press forward to his own solution, if indeed there were any solution at all. He took up position in the usual way beneath a tree, far from the world's distractions and far from the competing claims of rival religious leaders. We cannot precisely know the workings of his mind. But it was here that he settled all accounts with the universe in which he had found himself. When he finally arose he was able to explain the pattern of human existence to others in a way which helped them to an inward victory over its pains and limitations. This event was known as *bodhi*, meaning awakening or enlightenment and the place was called Bodh Gaya, suggesting *bodhi.* It is this key turning point of enlightenment or *bodhi* which, in retrospect, gives 'the Buddha' his title, both of these words being related to the same verbal root *budh,* meaning to awaken or to know. The tree under which he sat is therefore known as the *bodhi* tree, sometimes shortened to *bo* tree.

Although in one sense the Buddha's achievement was strictly personal, for it was the fruit of years of searching and effort, leading to a final balancing out of the problem of human existence, he was also able to speak of it to others. It included a perception of the character of experience, a special kind of knowledge therefore which could be declared and expounded in various ways. The Buddha did in fact make known the understanding at which he had arrived, meeting with varied responses. Although the places hitherto visited in his wanderings are not well attested it may reasonably be accepted that his first preaching activity took place at Benares. The precise form of his teaching can no longer be distinguished from its traditional rehearsal by generations of followers. We cannot even be sure that it included the famous formula of the 'four noble truths' (dealt with later in this book) because even this, like other summaries of Buddhist teaching, has its subsequent history within the tradition carried down by the monks. Nevertheless he certainly taught to the effect that human life is characterised by suffering and impermanence, that every action leads to consequences of some sort which are eventually unsatisfactory; but that it is possible to develop attitudes and behaviour which lead to freedom from our self-made chains.

He also gathered others about him, probably first admitting them to discipleship with the simple formula 'Come, monk!'. Gradually the rules of a community of homeless men were elaborated. Just as with accounts of the Buddha's teaching, it is no longer possible to be certain which elements of the lengthy books of discipline represent rules explicitly laid down by the Buddha in person. Some are sure to be elaborations intended to carry forward the spirit of the original style of life into new circumstances. However there was certainly a shared and increasingly organised discipline, with both individual and communal regulations. The men lived on offerings placed by others in their begging bowls and hence were called *bhikkhus,* which really means people who receive alms. Their clothing or 'robe' was made of cast-off pieces of cloth. They had no settled home, except that a sheltered retreat was allowed during the rainy season. Their rules were meant to discourage attachment to the passions. Four transgressions in particular required expulsion, namely sexual intercourse, thieving, taking human life (or inciting to suicide), and falsely claiming supernormal powers (whether spiritual states, or special abilities such as levitation). These and other rules were recited fortnightly at new moon and at full moon when members confessed their failures. It is likely that this practice, as well as the various stipulations contained within the ancient framework of discipline, are partly the result of the Buddha's personal influence and partly reflections of common practices among religious mendicants of the time. It is possible to see a common underlying pattern in the disciplinary codes of the various sects, but there is no historical information about sectarian variations until the time of the second council. This leaves an indefinite and unchartable period of gradual codification, after the Buddha himself had died. It is therefore impossible to assess to what extent and in what ways he personally was responsible for it during his lifetime.

There are so many references to other places in relatively old sources that we may be certain that the Buddha did not remain at Benares (or Varanasi). Well-known places which he visited are sure to include Rajagrha ('the King's house') where King Bimbisara of Magadha resided; Kapilavastu, which was the stronghold of the

Sakya people; Vaisali, the capital city of the Vrijjis; Sravasti, the capital of the Kosalas; and Kausambi, the capital of the Vatsa kingdom. The accounts of his journeys and residences cannot be turned into real history, for they are 'recorded' in very miscellaneous contexts, of interest to his followers long after. However it is clear that he gave teaching and advice freely to all kinds of people, whether they were villagers and merchants or kings and court officials. Patronage by the secular powers was also probably accepted within the Buddha's lifetime. This was the basis of the eventual development of Buddhism as a recognised and established religion, forming a third force alongside king (or state) and people, both in ancient India and later in other Buddhist countries.

We may assume that many wanderings and retreats were spread over an extended lifetime of teaching. A sustained cluster of narrative tells of the Buddha's last journeys and death, a sequence reserved in detail for later chapters. If we are historically restrained, we have to admit that much of it must be accounted legendary. Yet it irresistibly suggests an authoritative religious teacher, respected by his own personal followers such as Ananda and Mahakasyapa as well as by secular leaders and the general public. Whether he really died of a stomach infection, as a result of eating something disagreeable in a dish of pork prepared in good faith by a blacksmith, we shall never know. But he died of natural causes, self-confident, aged, revered – and mourned.

This initial account of the Buddha's personal story may seem to some to be indeed little but bare bones of history. Yet so much can be told without any reliance on miracle stories or even on those ever-growing legends where fact runs inextricably into fiction.

The next step is still by no means to plunge into the detailed elaborations of those full-length life stories of the Buddha composed long after, but to concentrate much more closely on the two clusters of narrative which were of central importance to the early Buddhists. The first deals with the Buddha's enlightenment and teaching; and the second is the account of his decease, known to the Buddhists as his nirvana. In taking this next step it will no longer be possible to consider whether each statement exactly reflects what happened in the same strict sense as hitherto. Similarly, the religious ideas and practices mentioned may not have been understood within the Buddha's historical lifetime precisely as we now have them before us. However, there is a good reason why these two clusters of narrative were particularly important to the early Buddhists. The reason is that the Buddha's enlightenment and his nirvana were models of what the Buddhists ultimately aimed at for themselves. In this sense they were the twin dynamos of Buddhism as a working religion. In considering these narratives next, we must recognise that we shall be one long stride removed from the original time. Nevertheless we shall not go far astray if it is along these lines that we build up our understanding of what happened. We shall be dependent on the two focal points of the early Buddhist recollection of the Buddha, which is a far cry from the fairy tales with which many books are littered.

PART TWO

ENLIGHTENMENT

3

Enlightenment

A common quest

Perhaps the most potent symbol of all Buddhism is the picture of the Buddha himself, newly enlightened, seated under the tree of enlightenment in a position of deep spiritual repose. This is the ultimate goal of all Buddhists for themselves since it leads naturally to nirvana. Admittedly the average Buddhist assumes that the way towards this goal is long and difficult, but nevertheless it has always been taken to be the main focal point of the Buddhist religion.

Initially the figure of the enlightened Buddha was important for two things which flowed from it. Firstly, it was the effective source of Buddhist teaching, and secondly it was the starting point of the Buddhist monastic order. In retrospect these two were added to the Buddha himself to make up the 'three jewels': Buddha, Dhamma and Samgha (Sanskrit: Dharma and Sangha). Since it was from the Buddha's experience under the tree of enlightenment that the teaching and the monastic community came into being, the first extended narratives of importance to the early Buddhists centred on the story of how this came about. It is striking that the story appears not only in the collection of sutras, but also, with some variation, in the books of monastic discipline (*vinaya*). This fact demonstrates very clearly that it was presumed to explain the very reason for the existence of Buddhist monastic discipline in the first place.

Many elaborate and legendary details were gradually built on to this narrative, especially in a long Sanskrit 'discipline' book called the *Mahavastu*, which in fact consists mainly of interpolated stories. As a matter of fact the parallels found in the *Mahavastu*, leaving aside all the obvious additions, have been found to confirm the existence of a relatively ancient common tradition. Nevertheless what follows below is mainly based on three related accounts in the Pali scriptures of Theravada Buddhism, all three of which are fairly restrained in their approach. Two of these narratives are sutras (called *suttas* in Pali), namely 'The Discourse on the Noble Quest' (*Ariyapariyesana Sutta*) and 'The Greater Discourse to Saccaka' (*Mahasaccaka Sutta*). The third is the opening part of the *Mahavagga* which is found in the canonical discipline books of the Theravada sect. These narratives are not simply reproduced here as texts, for the repetitions and allusions make them difficult to assimilate. However, the story is retold with the aim of bringing out the assumptions and the implications of the original, and interested readers can follow up the original texts for themselves.

In the books of discipline the narrative begins with the Buddha already seated under the tree of enlightenment and it takes the story further along than the sutras. The sutras begin at an earlier point and give information about the efforts which preceded the enlightenment. In both cases however the enlightenment is the central event which dominates the whole. Moreover 'The Discourse on the Noble Quest' ends with the teaching of five disciples, thus showing how Buddhism began; while the discipline narrative for its part assumes details of the Buddha's companions which are found in the sutra. Thus they complement each other, and both have the same basic *raison d'être* in providing a basis for the Buddhist community.

Early references to the Buddha's abandonment of home are relatively incidental, and they hardly form any part of the enlightenment narratives themselves. The commonly met statement is however that he left home to seek a state of being in which he would be free from rebirth, old age, sickness, death, sorrow and impurity. His parents grieved, we are told, to see their fine and healthy grown-up son cut off his deep black hair and put on the yellowish robe of a religious mendicant. But it was of no avail, for he was seeking the goal of freedom from the things which seemed to bind him. That goal was called in Pali *nibbana*, for which we use the now generally current Sanskrit equivalent: nirvana. Gotama first sought this state in the company of others, and it is here that the sutra narrative really begins to go into some detail. Two teachers of some repute are named, the first being Alara Kalama. The Buddha soon learned and inwardly appropriated his doctrine, which was said to lead to the realm of non-existence. Kalama recognised that he had done so and therefore offered to share the leadership of his band of monks with the Buddha. The latter considered however that attaining non-existence was not a sufficient answer to his search, and therefore went his way. The second such teacher whom he followed was named Uddaka, or alternatively Rama, because he was himself the disciple of another such teacher named Rama. The Buddha learned Uddaka's doctrine equally quickly, and assimilated it in his own experience. In this case it meant attaining a state of 'neither perception nor non-perception'. Uddaka realised the Buddha's achievement and, like Kalama, he proposed to share the leadership of his band of monks with him. However, just as before, the Buddha considered that such an attainment did not in itself solve the problem which he had set himself, and therefore went his way. The significance of this story is that the mental states referred to are two of the mental states known as *jhanas*, considered by Buddhists to be of limited value compared with enlightenment.

Wandering in the country of Maghada he had come to the town of Uruvela. Nearby he found a quiet forest place, with a clear stream for bathing and refreshing himself. There were villages where he would go to beg his food. It seemed a suitable place and so there he stayed.

It was at Uruvela that Gotama was accepted into the company of five other ascetics, who looked to him to achieve some new break-through which they might then adopt for themselves. This is not directly stated in all the narratives, but it is assumed in that the five are named as the eventual first recipients of his teaching. They encouraged him in the severe physical austerities which he now undertook. His self-mortification was of two kinds. Firstly he tried techniques of intense physical concentration to overcome the trouble in his mind, the most important being an attempt to maintain himself in trance while holding his breath, which proved to be very painful but not profitable. When he closed his mouth and nose the air passed through his ears with a violent sound. Probably this means that he burst an ear-drum. When he sealed his ears, his head pounded until he fell senseless. Secondly he tried taking food in quite minute amounts, just as much bean-juice or pieces of herbs as he could hold in the palm of his hand. Gradually he reduced himself to little more than skin and bone, his ribs protruded and his eyes in their hollowed sockets were little more than the sparkle of water at the bottom of deep wells. It is said that he could feel his spine through his stomach. When he moved from his position he fell from weakness and when he touched his discoloured limbs the hairs fell from their pores.

The point of these extreme descriptions was to show that Gotama went to the limit as far as yogic and ascetic practices were concerned. Another text, 'The Greater Lion's Roar Sutra' (*Mahasihanadasutta*) expands very greatly the list of austerities which he is said to have undertaken, obviously with the intention of making doubly sure that there is no known practice left by which the Buddha might find himself trumped. However, since these extreme measures did not bring about the desired result he eventually abandoned them and began to eat rice and sour milk given to him by villagers in the ordinary way. His companions thereupon took him to have given up altogether and so left him to his own devices. For Gotama, however, it was the path of sheer asceticism which had failed him, for although he had subdued his body to the utmost, the problem of birth and aging, disease and death still seemed to remain. His own resolve to break through to a solution was only steeled and refined by the failure of self-mortification as a method.

Such stories as these help to illustrate the religious culture of the time. On the one hand there was the Brahmanical system in which the religious specialists belonged to the hereditary Brahman caste, explained the universe as populated by various divinities, and performed community sacrifices in accordance with the calendar. On the other hand there were the wanderers, some teachers, some disciples, some just friends, living on the fringe of society, leading a simple life at the mercy of the climate, the wild beasts and the snakes, seeking to realise an inward balance and to learn or communicate spiritual practices or truths. It is in this latter culture that Gotama's enlightenment belongs.

Enlightenment

In 'The Discourse on the Noble Quest' there is no reference at all to the 'tree' of enlightenment. Gotama was simply seated in the pleasant spot he had found near Uruvela, and there he won the state of being which he had originally sought. We are not told how or why. Because he felt that he was in a state of bondage to birth, that is, rebirth, it meant that he was looking for 'the unborn'. This is one way of referring to nirvana. Such a state he is now declared to have achieved. Similarly he is no longer subject to age, to decay through sickness, to death, to sorrow or to impurity. These freedoms add up to nirvana. Thus the solution is stated in terms of a reversal of the problem, a typical characteristic of statements of Buddhist doctrine. He acquired 'knowledge' and 'vision'. Above all, the freedom from all the undesirable states which had troubled him was confirmed through his confidence that he would never again need to undergo rebirth.

It has been quite rightly stressed in earlier books that we find here no reference at all to a titanic struggle with the demon Mara, which plays such a prominent part in the later legend. Less attention has been paid to the important degree of variation even between the relatively discreet narratives which we are following at present. Only one of the three in any definite way describes the process of enlightenment. The plain fact is that we have no direct recording of it, and moreover, nor did the early generations of Buddhists. For this reason the gap is filled by a variety of meditational or doctrinal formulae which are equally well attested in other contexts – which were therefore, in one way and another, generally current. It is difficult to resist the view that the enlightenment narratives at this central point simply incorporate snatches of doctrine or meditational technique which were closely associated with the Buddha personally as a result of his constant teaching.

We have seen that in 'The Discourse on the Noble Quest', the 'content' of the enlightenment turned out simply to be, appropriately enough, a fulfilment of the quest defined on the occasion of Gotama's leaving home. In 'The Greater Discourse to Saccaka' however a more complex group of meditational achievements is set out, and as parts of it are repeated in other sutras too it is worthy of some attention.

The story follows on from Gotama's abandonment of fasting as a method, and the criticism of the five monks who had previously set their hopes on his leadership. After he took nourishment and gathered his strength, but without reverting to an ordinary dependence upon the comforts of the senses, he went into meditation again. The states of mind which he achieved are known as *dhyana* (*jhana* in Pali), and it is this Indian word which eventually became *ch'an* in Chinese and *zen* (of Zen Buddhism) in Japanese. What were these *dhyanas* or *zens*? Four are described in this context, each one leading into the next. The first allows reasoned thought to begin and to be followed through in the mind, and also gives rise to a sense of joyful elation. Secondly, the thought which has taken place is allowed to subside, and new mental activity is not initiated; the mind thus becomes tranquil and remains coherent through concentration on one single focus. The feeling of joyful elation is still present. Thirdly, this sense of rapture and elation is allowed to fade away through the attainment of an attitude of equanimity, a conscious balance unswayed by elation over the concentration of the mind. And fourthly, the equanimity so attained is applied retrospectively, so to speak, to the pleasures and pains of previous experience, thus balancing them all out and cancelling any further disturbing effects which they might have. In this state Gotama felt altogether purified by equanimity and, it should be noted, mindfulness.

Throughout this sequence he had felt himself to be in a state of well-being, not to be confused with the rush of elation consequent on controlling the mind, but a general pleasantness which did not disturb or influence his mind. The words *jhana* or *dhyana* are sometimes translated 'trance', but it is most important to notice that these states in no way involve a loss of control or awareness. On the contrary, the subject of the experience is in a position of full control and full awareness. He is not disturbed by any one particular train of thought or series of emotions. He is withdrawn from such entanglements, perfectly poised in a balance of fully conscious equanimity.

The four *jhanas* however do not themselves constitute the meaning of Gotama's enlightenment, even in those narratives in which they occur. They are equivalent to an athlete's preparatory fitness, not to the specific feat which he performs. If the *jhanas* are cognitively neutral, it is striking that the next step which Gotama took is described retrospectively in the narrative as a sequence of three kinds of 'knowledge'. This is of interest for two reasons. Firstly, it implies that the Buddha did not simply select some special type of spiritual practice from among the various alternatives of the time. On the contrary his enlightenment had some relationship, it was presumed, to the very character of the universe, and the account of his enlightenment consists in part at least of a statement about the way things are. It is not an abstract or casual analysis however, but one related to the initially problematic quality of life and the resolution of the problem. In this respect, all three narratives are agreed, even though they fill out the story with completely different traditional formulae.

'The Greater Discourse to Saccaka' continues then with three kinds of knowledge. What are these three? The first of them is the Buddha's recollection of his own previous existences, which all became visible to him during the first watch of the night. The idea behind this is that when he was in the fourth *jhana* his mind was no longer confined and conditioned by the thought and emotions of the moment, but was such an unshakeably clear yet flexible instrument that it could be directed towards any part of human experience, like, we might say today, some great and powerful searchlight. This 'knowledge' of previous existences of course assumes also that the forces constituting individual life work on indefinitely, reconstituting themselves again and again in new circumstances. Thus the Buddha remembered his former lives. Not just a few did he recall, but hundreds and hundreds, indeed a hundred thousand, to give a round number. He remembered the name, the clan, the colour of his skin, his livelihood, his experiences pleasant and painful, and the length of his life. Particular lives are not mentioned at all in these narratives; such details were left to the endless imagination of later Buddhists. The meaning of this knowledge, couched as it is in terms of the idea of karma and rebirth, is that the Buddha had a thorough perception of how he had come to be as he was, through an immensely long series of generations. He recognised his own conditioning and in this sense 'ignorance was dispelled' and 'light arose'. His previous experience and present standpoint was entirely clear to him. It was, one might say, the absolute fulfilment in Indian terms of the Greek injunction 'Know thyself!'.

The second knowledge was achieved in the second watch of the night, and was a universal form of the first. Now the light was turned on to the coming to be and the passing away of all kinds of living beings. The ability to see all this is called *deva*-vision, or, as we might transpose it, angel-vision. All the many inhabitants of the universe were apparent to him in their various conditions of well-being and misery, beauty and ugliness, good fortune or bad, depending on the karmic value of their deeds. Those who thought and spoke and acted wrongly were reborn in a sad place of torment, while those who acquitted themselves with virtue found themselves, in their next birth, in a heavenly realm. These first two 'knowledges' are presented as offering an integrated understanding of all experience to date, an understanding not naturally open to everybody, but part of the Buddha's own personal break-through in respect of the problem of human existence.

The third 'knowledge', achieved not surprisingly in the third watch of the night, was the knowledge that he was indeed finally free. 'Knowledge of the destruction of the cankers' is the phrase used in Miss I. B. Horner's important translation of 'The Middle Length Sayings', but the rather unusual word 'canker' needs to be explained. The original word is *asava* (Sanskrit: *asrava*), and it has also been translated regularly by Edward Conze as 'outflow'. The root of the word means such things as 'flow', 'trickle' or 'ooze' and Miss Horner selected the word 'canker' as an English translation on the basis of its meaning as 'anything that frets, corrodes, corrupts or consumes slowly and secretly' (*Oxford English Dictionary*). What are the three cankers? They are sense-pleasures, coming into being (becoming), and ignorance. How these ooze and trickle from us all, stocking up the forces which feed the sufferings of the next generation, and the next, and the next! 'Knowledge of the cankers' is the shorthand formula for a form of understanding related to the famous 'four noble truths'. These are introduced in the enlightenment narrative in the lightest possible way, at this point, and they figure more prominently in the Buddha's post-enlightenment teaching. Just as the Buddha perceived suffering, the arising of suffering, the stopping of suffering and the way to bring about the stopping of suffering (that is, the four noble truths), so he perceived the cankers, their arising, their stopping and the way of stopping them. The three cankers all have the same logical position in this scheme as is taken up by suffering. In so thoroughly understanding the interrelations of all these factors, the Buddha found that his mind was no longer in any way controlled by them. He was freed from the sense-pleasures, freed from the constant round of coming into being, and of course through this pervasive understanding of human existence he no longer oozed ignorance. With this sense of freedom came the realisation that there was nothing within him to bring about a further birth, the great journey which he had pursued through so many existences had reached its end, and all that was to be done had been done.

An idle reading of the narratives might suggest that it was merely a question of acquiring a certain kind of knowledge, after which the problem of life turns out to be self-resolving. This would mean that the Buddhist path is open to intellectuals only, and that by virtue of their mental powers such people can easily follow on to the condition which the Buddha himself achieved. Nothing could be further from the truth. Remember that the Buddha acquired these perceptions on the basis of complete equanimity and self-awareness in a moral and meditational sense. Though his mind was clear, it was not rippled by intellectual attachments or enthusiasms, both of which characterise intellectuals as such. Moreover the three 'knowledges' were not just 'known' in a limited cognitive sense. They were existentially appropriated into the Buddha's own condition of life, which, he saw, was at last no longer productive of karma. Hence the clarity of enlightenment entailed cessation (*nirodha*) or nirvana.

Why did the Buddha not thereupon disappear into thin air or empty space, one might perhaps ask; and indeed the ancient tradition puts the same question when puzzled enquirers wanted to know why it is that the Buddha still went off to meditate by himself, and indeed still needed to take sleep. The answer was simply that the final physical body had its course to run. Meditation is relaxing, and a good example to others. As to sleep, the Buddha even admitted that he sometimes took a nap during the day-time; not, to be sure, in a confused and careless way like so many of us lazy humans, but only on purpose, towards the end of the hot season, after his meal of begged food, folding up his outer robe into four, and lying down on his right side. When the cankers have been cut off, they are like the stump of a palm tree which cannot produce new shoots. This means that a Buddha, or a Tathagata, calmly finishes off all the rest of his physical life, without fear of producing any new karma for the future. On death, the body will dissolve and in that final nirvana no karma will remain.

Meditation on Causal Arising

We have already seen two complementary versions of Gotama's attainment of enlightenment. A third, the *Mahavagga* account in the books of discipline, has its own contribution to make. Here the first part called the 'Tale of Enlightenment' (*Bodhi-katha*) does begin with the Buddha seated quite specifically under the 'tree of enlightenment' (*bodhirukkha*), near the river Neranjara, in the neighbourhood of Uruvela. He was seated cross-legged, that is, in a simple yoga position which trained persons find relaxing, and so he remained for 'seven' days in enjoyment of the freedom which he had attained. As in 'The Discourse on the Noble Quest' there is no explanation of the process by which he attained enlightenment, though of course in this case the narrative does assume some things referred to above which were preserved in the sutras. For example it transpires later that the Buddha wishes to return to his previous teachers and companions, though the story does not begin with any account of these. It is notable that here too there is no elaboration of any battle with the mythical Mara, although one verse quoted in the story has an incidental reference to it, and this may illustrate how the story came to be worked in much later. What is certainly assumed is that within the range of possible practices and ideas the Buddha struck a particular note in his own personal experience, concentrated in solitude, after whittling down the issues though the rejection of various apparently blind alleys. Thus the recently enlightened Buddha is seated beneath the *bo* tree in a state of freedom or release (*vimutti*). The meaning of this state of release, and thus the meaning of the Buddha's enlightenment, is indicated when his meditation is described in a well-known formula.

This formula, which may be known for convenience as Causal Arising, is found in so many ancient Buddhist texts that we may think of it as one of the persistent threads out of which the whole system was woven. On the other hand we should remember that it appears in various forms in these different places, and it is not possible to refine these down directly into the surely known words of the historical Buddha himself. The *Mahavagga* gives it in a very common but presumably not the most archaic form, consisting of twelve mutually conditioning factors of existence. In this formula the first quality of human existence is ignorance, upon which there rears up the whole structure of physical and mental life: mental constituents (item 2 in the formula), consciousness (3), mind and body (4) and the six senses (5). These items may seem in translation to overlap with each other, but the original terms represent well-established patterns by which the ancient Indians could easily articulate their understanding of human psychology. The list continues by relating the individual to the outside world through contact (6), feeling (7) desire (8) and grasping (9), a steady sequence of enmeshment in things. Finally this whole account of human nature issues in the full reality of an individual existence through 'becoming' (10), which implies conception, birth itself (11) and what that in turn entails, namely old age and death (together making item 12). It is difficult to read the formula as a precise causal chain throughout, though each item is supposed to condition the next. Probably it is wrong to see it as a doctrinal or theoretical argument. Indeed it is presented rather as a meditational sequence, to which the Buddha paid attention during the first watch of the night. Each item spot-lights one aspect of human existence, but taken together they bowl along the entire rush of human striving. Because the outcome of every new pressure into existence is old age and death, the keynote of the whole is suffering and sorrow. The meditation offers an overall pattern of self-understanding related to the problem with which the Buddha had originally set out on his path.

The same series can also be rehearsed the other way round, and the meditation during the first watch of the night consisted of moving through the whole list first one way and then the other way. In practice the text being followed here does not reverse the list but changes the relation from conditioning to simultaneous cessation. This means that ignorance ceasing leads to mental constituents ceasing, and so on, up to birth ceasing and old age with death ceasing. Thus just as the whole series in direct order indicates the interconnected arising of the whole network of suffering, so the series in reverse indicates the cessation (*nirodha*) of the very same. The arising of it all begins with ignorance, but the ending of ignorance leads to the passing away of the problem. Although the cessation of ignorance is given here as a negative concept it is not surprising that the Buddha's attainment was also termed 'all-knowledge'. This is not to be understood as knowing a huge number of miscellaneous pieces of information, which would be a particularly bad case of 'ignorance' in Buddhist terms, but rather a pervasive and interconnected perception of the character of individual existence: how it arises, in all its suffering, and how it ceases.

The formula of Causal Arising has been explained and used in many ways. One of the most interesting, though not the work of the Buddha himself, is the allegorical presentation of the twelve items in a wheel which also depicts the various conditions in which new births or 'rebirths' can take place.

The Buddha himself is described as reviewing Causal Arising, in direct and reverse order, during the first watch of the night. Then he made a solemn declaration that all things were clear to him, and repeated the meditation in the middle watch, and again in the last watch. After the last watch he added, according to a verse embedded in the story, that the army of Mara was thereby defeated. Mara is the evil tempter who with all his helpers tries to deflect the Buddha from his path. However it should be remembered that in this narrative the meaning of what happened at the Buddha's enlightenment is given almost entirely in terms of the meditation on Causal Arising. It is one more alternative way, like the two considered earlier, of narrating Gotama's achievement. The combined evidence of the three is that it was both a spiritual victory for him personally, and the matrix of an analysis of human existence which has reverberated whenever Buddhist doctrine has been taught.

As to the *Mahavagga* narrative itself, the opening scene of the Buddha seated under the Bodhi tree, in meditation on Causal Arising, turns out to be the prologue to further inward reflections on the Buddha's part, and to various conversations with others. It is a point of initiation with respect to all that came after.

4

Reflections and Meetings

First encounters

There was still no following of disciples for this independent hermit who had abandoned the methods of his contemporaries to find release in his own way. After the crisis he continued to sit in meditation beneath suitable trees. One was a banyan tree frequented by goatherds, presumably for the shade of its vast rooting branches. After sitting here cross-legged for 'seven days' as before, he was approached respectfully by an otherwise unknown Brahman whose special religious practice consisted of chanting the syllable *hum*. On asking the Buddha what he should do to live as a Brahman, he was told to abandon chanting *hum-hum* and to concentrate on eliminating moral impurities. This, together with a thorough knowledge of the *Vedas*, the ancient holy texts of India, would allow him rightly to claim the title of Brahman. Although the Buddha neither expounded his own teaching, nor made the Brahman a disciple, it is evident that in his reply he disregarded both hereditary religion and mindless ritual in favour of inward discipline. After years spent in the forest perhaps this is not surprising, but the encounter sums up the general attitude of the Buddha towards traditional Hindu religion.

The next tree under which the Buddha is supposed to have sat, for a further seven days, is named Mucalinda after a mythical serpent king. As the weather was unusually stormy this great serpent is said to have appeared from his haunts and wrapped his coils around the Buddha, seven times of course, to protect him from the elements, whether wind, heat, flies, etc. After the seven days the Buddha is credited with another solemn pronouncement about the value of arresting desires and self-assertion. Unlike the encounter with the Brahman, it is difficult to see what biographical reality could have given rise to this story, except in so far as the newly enlightened Buddha was in a state of such psychological ease and balance as to be quite oblivious to severe variations in the weather.

From there he moved on to a tree of unknown variety named the Rajayatana tree, possibly in reminiscence of a place-name. The story is in stereotype, for again he remained seated cross-legged under this tree for seven days. This time however he was approached by two travelling merchants named Tapussa and Bhallika, who had been told of the holy man seated beneath the tree. They approached and greeted him, and then offered him nourishing food made with barley and honey. As they offered it they expressed the desire that this would bring them blessing for the future, thus stating the principle upon which all later relations between monks and laymen were to rest: an offering of physical necessities in exchange for a spiritual reward, credit, or merit. The ancient narrative shows us the mythical great kings of the four quarters of the compass each giving the Buddha a brand new bowl made of rock-crystal for this occasion. The point of this is to stress that the Buddha did not just receive the food in his hands but in an ordered manner, solemnly befitting this first gift of food. The story symbolises a kind of compact, made by the Buddha with the very first people to offer him food. In a sense this simple act of giving and receiving has been continued through the monastic community down to the present day.

When the Buddha had eaten the food the merchants spoke to him again and, with a bow, they formally requested him to accept them as his followers. We must distinguish here between a lay disciple (*upasaka*), which is what the merchants now became, and an almsman or monk (*bhikkhu*) who leaves the ordinary world of commerce and household life. Since there was as yet no monastic community Tapussa and Bhallika were made lay disciples through the two-fold formula of going for refuge to the Buddha (here referred to as Bhagava, or Lord) and to the Dhamma or 'teaching'. There is no indication as yet of what the Dhamma was, and so behind the artificialities of the narrative some exchanges on this subject have to be presumed. On the other hand laymen do not necessarily receive extensive teaching and the Buddha's encounters were so far quite incidental to his own blissful seclusion at the foot of various trees.

The decision to teach

Still alone, the Buddha returned to the banyan tree, but now he began to weigh up the courses of action open to him. In his mind he saw the great gulf between the Dhamma on one hand and ordinary, ignorant humanity on the other hand. The Dhamma seemed both subtle and peaceful, the recognition of Causal Arising being difficult to explain, and the stopping of attachment and craving, leading to nirvana, being hard to achieve. Since people were so entranced with sensual pleasures they would scarcely understand and follow the Dhamma, and any attempt to teach it would merely be pointless and wearisome. For this reason, to use the immortal phrase in Miss Horner's translation, 'his mind inclined to little effort'. If things had rested there the reception of Tapussa's and Bhallika's homage would have remained a casual incident and the Buddhist religion would never have been founded. The Buddha would have remained just another hermit wearing rags and eating scraps, spending his time meditating under trees, eventually passing away unknown and unmourned.

The pious may treat what happened next as a supernatural intervention. So indeed the narrative presents it when the great god Brahma, also named Sahampati, disappeared from his ordinary place in the heavens and in the twinkling of an eye came to stand before the Buddha. In effect, the other side of the argument in the Buddha's own mind is presented to us in the form of a vision, in the language of ancient India. The god greets the Buddha in the conventional way, robe over one shoulder, right knee dropped to the ground, hands joined in salutation, and then pleads with him to teach the Dhamma. What is the argument on the other side? It is that although some will fail to understand there are nevertheless others who could learn and grow if they were to hear. Without being taught they will also decline. The Buddha himself is like a man standing on a mountain-top, looking down on all the people still bound by suffering. He should step forward and teach, for the sake of those who would benefit.

To this vision the Buddha replied with his original argument, only to be entreated a second time, and a third time. A threefold entreaty is never without result, as all the world's literature knows. Finally therefore the Buddha looked across the whole world, with the eye of a Buddha, seeing into the hearts and minds of all the people, good and bad, sharp and dull, aware and blinded. Just like lotuses they seemed, some growing in the water, quite immersed, others reaching up to the surface, and others growing in the water but rising up to flower above it. His decision made, he addressed the visionary god once more, declaring that 'the deathless' was henceforward open to any who would hear him. The word 'nirvana' has been used earlier, meaning a cessation of all those things involved in Causal Arising. 'The deathless' is another term for the state attained by a Buddha, meaning however not immortality in the sense of a mere continuation of life as presently lived, but release from the otherwise never-ending cycle of birth and death and rebirth. This inward resolve of the Buddha, though presented in a mythologised form, was a crucial hinge in the narrative leading from his enlightenment to the founding of the Buddhist religion. There also seems no reason to doubt that he did, some time after his own attainment of peacefulness of mind, go through an experience of uncertainty, and then decision, about whether to try to share his attainment with his fellow-men.

It is all very well for a Buddha to see the inward dispositions of men and women all over the world with his 'Buddha-eye', some of whom might listen favourably to the new teaching. But the practical reality must have seemed different. It is hard for us now to imagine an Asia, even an India, with all its towns and villages and roadways, merchants, kings, scoundrels, beggars and villagers, a population without end – but no Buddhism. Where was he to begin? According to the narrative he wished to teach first to those who would understand him quickly, and his thoughts turned to those former teachers Alara Kalama and Uddaka the pupil of Rama. The human reality asserts itself again, for he found that both men had passed away while he was still meditating under the trees. In the narrative invisible angels report it to him: Alara had died seven days ago, and Uddaka just the night before. The poignancy lies in his wish to report to representatives of the older tradition from which he had learned, too late. The next to turn to should be the five hermits in whose company he had practiced asceticism. They were presently staying at Isipatana near Varanasi (Benares), and so the Buddha set off there from Uruvela. Although the narrative sometimes credits the Buddha with special powers, e.g. in knowing the whereabouts of the five hermits, it appears that as far as getting there is concerned he had to walk, in the ordinary way.

Again we are confronted with real life, for the main event on his journey was an utterly fruitless encounter with another wandering ascetic. This was Upaka, who is described as an *ajivika*. Unfortunately little is known about the ajivikas and their relations with other sects such as the ascetic Jains or the Achelakas. It is not even clear whether they were a definite sect, or whether the word simply referred to men who lived independently as begging ascetics. They are also sometimes known as 'naked ascetics'. Upaka met the Buddha on the road near Bodh Gaya and noticed that he seemed particularly clear of complexion. He greeted him respectfully and asked him, in the way such travellers did, who his teacher was or what his Dhamma was. The Buddha replied in words of incomparable self-assurance that he was victorious, omniscient, teacher-less and unequalled among gods and men. He alone was completely enlightened. He had attained nirvana. Upaka replied, perhaps ironically, that he certainly sounded as if he had conquered 'the unending'; with which the Buddha did not hesitate to agree. Upaka was unconvinced. 'That may be so,' he said, and off he went down another road, shaking his head.

It is not at all clear why this story was included in the Buddhist narrative. Later pietists tried to claim that Upaka eventually repented and became the Buddha's disciple just before he died. As it stands however the point of the story seems to lie in the contrast between the Buddha's prodigious claims, and Upaka's experienced response. He had heard of many teachers, no doubt. They all had their Dhamma. He was impressed by the Buddha's confident appearance, but could not bring himself to expect very much more. There may have been something in what the Buddha said, but then again there may not. What devastating incredulity.

Eventually the Buddha arrived at Varanasi where the five monks were staying in the deer park. This time human psychology worked the other way round. The monks saw him coming and reminded each other that it was the Gotama who had once striven with them to subdue the body but who had then abandoned the exercise. They decided that he should not be received back into their company, though he might be allowed to sit down nearby. As the Buddha came nearer, their resolve weakened, and one by one they made him welcome after all. They took his bowl and his robe, made him sit down and let him wash his feet, addressing him with terms of common respect.

Upon this the Buddha told them of his experience and claimed recognition of his enlightenment. The monks were once more sceptical. They failed to use the new and higher title of Tathagata, which implies the status of Buddha-hood, and which the narrative makes the Buddha claim for himself. After all, they argued, Gotama had not arrived at this exalted knowledge when he practised austerities, so why should they believe that he had done so when he reverted to ordinary ways of living? The Buddha retorted that a Tathagata was not one who had reverted to a life of abundance, giving up the quest for self-mastery. And he repeated his claim to have reached perfected enlightenment and to have found 'the deathless'. The other monks should hear his teaching, and they too would arrive at the goal which they sought when they first left home. Still the monks demurred, and as the narrative gives human truth in story form, the argument is repeated three times. Finally the Buddha makes them admit that he had never talked in such a way before, and that he therefore really did have something to say. So they decided to hear him out. Although by this time he had already trodden quite a few miles and spoken not a few thoughts, we come now to what is usually known as the Buddha's first teaching, or more picturesquely, the first rolling of the wheel of Dhamma.

5

Teaching the Five Monks

The middle way

One of the oldest symbols of Buddhism is the wheel, and sometimes it is represented together with deer, representing the Isipatana deer park near Benares where the Buddha's teaching was first effectively expounded. The reader already has by now some acquaintance with the Buddha's doctrine, from the accounts of the enlightenment itself, although of course there is no implication in the texts that these were public knowledge at the time. In his meeting with Upaka the Buddha only got as far as proclaiming that he had emerged victorious, and Upaka had departed before he had any opportunity to expound his new-found Dhamma, or teaching. Now it is the five monks known for their belief in the value of asceticism to whom he speaks, and it is a striking indication of the nature of Buddhist thought that what he says does not repeat *any* of the enlightenment narratives given earlier. Instead the Buddha expresses himself in terms of the problem which exercises the five monks, namely that Gotama seemed to have given up the ascetic striving in which they had encouraged him, and yet has the nerve to come back and claim to have found 'the deathless'.

There are two dead ends in the religious life, he argued. The first is a low, boorish addiction to sense-pleasures such as the average man is always guilty of. Such addiction is not *aryan*, that is, not noble, and it has nothing to do with the goal of the homeless wanderers. One may imagine the five monks nodding their heads, or more probably wagging their heads from side to side in Indian fashion, showing their agreement and relief at this promising start. But the other blind alley is addiction to ascetic practices, in other words addiction to precisely that on which they had formerly set their hopes. Such fanatical dependence on self-mortification was equally ignoble and equally irrelevant to their quest. Between these two false roads lay a middle way however, to which the Buddha himself was fully committed, a way which led to knowledge of the truth and to calming of the passions, in short to enlightenment and to nirvana. The Buddha's own perception of this way provides its normative characterisation. It was his own experience of abandoning ascetic practice, and yet by no means reverting to attachment to the sense-pleasures of eating, washing and so on for their own sakes, which indicates where the middle way lies. Thus it remained his responsibility to declare in more detail of what it consisted.

Here we come to another of the most famous formulae of Buddhism, impossible not to consider in the context of the religious founder himself, yet associated with him by the rather tenuous historical thread of the devotion of countless followers, namely 'the noble eight-fold path'. The eight aspects of this path are something of a mixture, and it may be helpful to show how the early Buddhists divided them up, even though these divisions do not appear in the *Mahavagga* narrative. The divisions are found in a kind of catechism, canonical in status, but appropriately entitled *The Lesser Discourse on the Miscellany.*

Item in Eightfold Path	*Classification*
right view right thought	knowledge or wisdom
right speech right action right mode of life	morality
right effort right awareness right concentration	concentration (meditation)

This bare list may make it appear rather like saying that if one takes the right road one will arrive at the intended destination, and indeed the list is not further explained in the story of the Buddha's teaching. Clearly it is used in the narrative as a convenient summary of many details in the Buddhist way of life which are presumed to have been enjoined by the Buddha. However, the three types of item already say a great deal about the character of Buddhism. We may project back the historical probability that the Buddha continued to value techniques of spiritual self-gathering and purification. He did not offer some such new technique, but presupposed concentration techniques as a peasant tills the ground. Secondly, his teaching was not lacking in moral requirements, although admittedly these were put on the basis of the advantage or disadvantage accruing to the disciple himself, rather than on any concerns independent of that individual's destiny. Thirdly, there was also a cognitive element. The middle way includes a right understanding of human existence. Wrong views lead to lack of progress. Thus we see that the Buddha's teaching was neither anti-intellectual nor anti-moral. On the other hand it was important for intellectual and moral endeavour to be shaped towards the goal of release or nirvana. The Buddha was not interested in their possible general validity outside the framework of that intention.

The 'noble truths'

The eightfold path is closely followed by 'the four noble truths' mentioned earlier in passing. These centre around the common theme of 'suffering' or 'ill', the underlying unsatisfactoriness of life which had formed Gotama's original problem. Again, although it would be foolhardy not to speak of the four noble truths in the context of the Buddha himself, it is in fact quite impossible to prove that he ever uttered them. Might one say, with great care, that the four noble truths state what the Buddha taught? If so, what is it that they state? The first truth 'the noble truth of suffering' declares that human experience is characterised by suffering: birth, old age, disease, dying, all these add up to a continuous cycle of suffering. Moreover finding oneself together with unpleasant things, or being separated from the pleasant things, or just not getting what one wants, these also contribute to the unsatisfactoriness of everything. Or finally, 'the five grasping constituents', which go to make up the individual as we know him, are characterised by suffering. The text assumes knowledge of what these five constituents are, which proves either that his hearers already knew them and therefore the Buddha was not the first to formulate them historically; or that the text was stitched together out of what he was later known to have taught. Either way, it is a reminder, if such is still necessary, that we are not dealing with an exact reminiscence close to the time, but with a composite tradition. The five 'constituents' themselves will be referred to again later, for they reappear in another context.

The second is 'the noble truth of the arising of suffering', which is brought about by craving or desire. This means above all craving for the pleasures of the senses (*kama-tanha*) or craving for further existence (*bhava-tanha*), but it also includes the more elusive concept of craving for dis-becoming (*vibhava-tanha*). This seems to suggest that an attachment to the idea of getting out of suffering is self-defeating. Desperately to seek it means that one is still controlled by desire for pleasant states. It is perhaps relevant to note that suicide is not considered a solution to life's problems in Buddhism, for the simple reason that it would only lead to another birth. The same applies to craving for 'dis-becoming'.

The third is 'the noble truth of the cessation of suffering'. This cessation (*nirodha*) is brought about by the giving up of craving. Just as in the meditation on Causal Arising, if the logic of the arising of suffering is put into reverse, in experience of course, not just as a mental trick, then this will lead to the cessation of suffering.

The fourth is 'the truth of the course which leads to the cessation of suffering'. Since it is not just an intellectual flip, practical steps are needed to put the logical reversal into effect. These practical steps are the eightfold path, which is repeated as before.

In the Buddha's speech, the recognition of these four truths is then declared to have been the form of his enlightenment experience. So once again the narrative provides another alternative formula of Buddhist teaching to depict that central event. In effect it is treated as a meditation in itself, for each truth is considered in three ways: firstly as being indeed true, secondly as demanding an existential response, and thirdly as having been so appropriated in experience. Before Gotama had achieved a purified vision of each of the resulting twelve lines of meditation, he was, the text recites, not yet enlightened. But when this full vision of knowledge became his, then he *was* enlightened, and thoroughly understood the world with all its varied inhabitants, its gods, men and demons. With this perfected vision he knew that he was now in his last round of existence, and that his freedom was at last assured. Thus the first teaching is clearly represented as flowing directly from the enlightenment experience. To put it historically, it was passed on among the generations of monks who followed after the Buddha's own life, that his enlightenment consisted of an inward, spiritual appropriation of the teaching expressed in the formula of the four noble truths.

First ordinations

The *Mahavagga* narrative, being already rather elaborated in the tradition, speaks of angelic voices and an earthquake at this point, but we shall leave such matters until later. At the same time, we hear that one of the five monks, named Kondanna, himself realised while the Buddha spoke that 'whatever arises also ceases', which is the nub of many central formulations of the Buddha's teaching. The Buddha realised this and gave him the additional name of Annata which means 'he who has understood'. Annata Kondanna was therefore the first person to recognise the meaning of the Buddha's teaching or 'Dhamma'. Having no more doubts in his mind he requested the Buddha to ordain him, or, that is, to be formally recognised as renouncing ordinary life in the Buddha's presence. There were as yet no regulations for entering the religious order which eventually came into being, and so he was received with the simple formula 'Come, monk!' (*ehi bhikkhu*), and the accompanying words, 'Well taught is Dhamma; follow the supreme way (*Brahma-cariya*) for making a complete end of suffering.'

Although the other four monks soon followed suit, this apparently did not happen automatically; and in this we may perceive the human history behind the semi-ritualised narrative. First two of the others, named Vappa and Bhaddiya, sought ordination, and thereafter they went with Kondanna on a begging mission. Although it is only mentioned incidentally, this alms-seeking procedure was another vital element in the founding of the Buddha's religious order. While he continued to instruct the remaining two monks, he did so on the basis that all six would live on the food brought back by the three others. The implication of this is that they formed a corporate brotherhood. Before long the other two ascetics recognised the authority of the Buddha's teaching and were ordained in the same way as the first three.

In this way all the basic ingredients of the Buddhist religion are closely and firmly related to the story of Gotama's own enlightenment. He was recognised to be 'the Buddha', his Dhamma was proclaimed and accepted as authoritative, and the corporate life of the monks, or *bhikkhus*, based on the collection of alms from the lay populace, was the basis of what was then known as the Samgha (Sanskrit: Sangha).

Non-self

The teaching of the four noble truths is traditionally described as the Buddha's 'first utterance', his first 'turning of the wheel of Dhamma' at the deer park in Benares. It was no doubt soon followed by many of the other expositions of his teaching which have been transmitted, and elaborated, in the whole literature of the Buddhist sutras. It will suffice here to restrict ourselves to one other piece of teaching, narrated in the *Mahavagga* at this point as being given to the same five monks in the deer park. This teaching was about the well-known and often puzzling idea of 'non-self', which through the centuries has continued to be a constant thread in Buddhist doctrine. It differs from the summaries of 'Dhamma' given above, in not appearing to be thought of as part of the Buddha's own enlightenment process. On the other hand it is typical of much of the Buddha's presumed teaching in taking the form of a dialogue with his monks, intended step by step to weed out false views and to leave room for a right perception of things.

In explaining the first of the noble truths the phrase 'five grasping constituents' (*panc' upadanakkhandha*) was used, and these five constituents now play a more important part. Together they form a comprehensive analysis of the individual as we ordinarily know him, covering both physical and psychological aspects.

The five are known as: body, feeling, perception, mental factors (or 'habitual tendencies') and consciousness. Although not explained in the narrative, it is assumed that it is these five which channel the karmic forces which make up the individual in one life, and which then are reassembled to form another individual in a subsequent life, and so on. However, there is no central organising principle apart from these, which could be thought of as independent of them, and which might have some spiritual destiny of its own. Thus the Buddha taught that there is no such thing as a disembodied soul, or for that matter a soul beyond our ordinarily constituted consciousness. There is no immune spiritual principle within to which one might flee from ordinary experience.

The argument itself is based on the presupposition that the five 'constituents' do in fact provide a comprehensive analysis of individuality. Body or form (*rupa*) does not provide us with such a self or soul, for it is subject to sickness beyond the control of the individual. The same is true for feeling and perception, and for the mental factors and consciousness. All of these are subject to decay and cannot be controlled at will. So the Buddha states it. Then the disciples are catechised. Is the body permanent or impermanent? The monks answer that it is impermanent. Are impermanent things satisfactory or subject to suffering? – the questioner continues. Of course, the answer is that they are subject to suffering. Is it right to think of what is impermanent and subject to suffering and decay as constituting a 'self' or 'soul'? And the answer given is no. So the catechism went on, with the same three questions being put with respect to the other four constituents, up to consciousness. Then the monks were exhorted, again in a five-fold routine, to see each of the five 'as it really is' namely as not permanently owned and not constituting a self. In this way, the Buddha concluded, the disciples should disregard the body etc. and through not seeking in these constituents a permanent self they would be freed from the pressure to be reborn again and again. During this talk the five monks are all said to have been freed from the 'cankers' (explained earlier) and to have reached a state of being *arahants* (Sanskrit: *arhats*), or, that is, 'perfected ones'.

Westerners who read about Buddhism are often puzzled over how it is that people are reborn or reincarnated if there is no invisible soul to move on from one life to the next. This problem is brought about by the associations of slightly non-Buddhist ideas. Whether right or wrong, the Buddhist teaching is in fact quite straightforward. Human existence is interpreted in terms of a cluster of forces, that is, the five constituents, which at any given time add up to one individual. When this individual, who like everything else is subject to change and decay, comes to the end of his life, the same forces which he himself has whipped forward by his own desires and actions regroup themselves to form another individual, who is born in circumstances reflecting whatever has been left over from before. This does not mean that any one of the constituent factors is itself permanent or unchanging. On the contrary, each is subject to flux and can in principle be allowed to die down altogether. Rebirth is not conceived of as being a good thing. On the contrary it is thought of as something which ought eventually to be avoided. However, most people are far from that goal of perfection or arahantship, and therefore it is sensible to hope for a 'better' birth in the future, a happier birth perhaps, but above all a birth which will give a greater likelihood of eventual release from all suffering. This conception is not spelled out in so many words in the text which has been followed immediately above, but it is the underlying premise and continuous accompaniment of the teaching about non-self. It is possible that this teaching, named *anatta* (or Sanskrit *anatman*) was directed particularly against the religious ideas of the Hindu *Upanishads*, and though this is not explicitly stated there is certainly a conflict of teaching at this point.

The Buddha's teaching was certainly not the same as just any other teaching. It had its own specific direction and style. Not being attached to the passions and not being attached to asceticism was matched by an intellectual version of 'the middle way' which refused to allow attachment to either nihilist or eternalist thought. The Buddha's thought ranged about and within the impermanent world of experience itself, with the intention of clarifying the path to release. This intellectual activity, with both its intention and its style, was a gift of the Buddha to subsequent generations of monks.

6

Ordinations and Rules

Ordinations at Benares

Once the Buddha's teaching was launched and a small band of loyal disciples had accepted his authority the way was open for a much wider development of what became, in effect, the Buddhist religion. The narratives which centre on the enlightenment experience itself have been seen to overlap in important ways, but now it is necessary to follow the account given in the *Mahavagga* alone, to see how it leads into the endless casuistry of the monastic discipline. There are several stories to tell. In the original narrative, legendary elaboration is clearly evident which will not be surveyed in detail here. However the stories all refer to people who came to be ordained into the Buddha's order or were accepted as lay disciples. While particular details must be declared uncertain in a historical sense, there seems to be no doubt that there were such persons who accrued to the Buddha's following.

The first of these stories is about the son of a rich merchant in Benares, named Yasa. He had no less than three villas at his disposal for cold, hot and rainy seasons respectively. During the rainy season he was entertained with music by bands of girls, so that the time passed pleasantly away. They also formed his harem with whom he slept each night. One night, after being pandered to in every possible way, he fell asleep before his companions and therefore woke first. Everybody was sleeping around in various dishevelled positions, with their musical instruments askew, and Yasa felt such a sense of disgust at this sight that he got up quietly and put on his golden shoes and stole out of the house. Down the street and out of the city he went, and off to the deer park of Isipatana. It was just before dawn. The Buddha was already awake and had seen him coming. When the young man had respectfully approached the Buddha began to teach him about the folly of slavery to the passions and told him of the four truths of suffering, its arising, its stopping and the way. In the meantime Yasa had been missed. His mother told his father; his father sent off messengers in all directions, and then himself followed his son's footprints to the deer park. At first the Buddha concealed Yasa's presence – by sheer psychic power the story says – and began to instruct Yasa's father as well. The latter was so impressed that he requested acceptance as a lay disciple, and did so with the formula of taking refuge in the Buddha, the Dhamma and the Samgha, the Buddha, his teaching, and the order of monks. This threefold formula is stressed by the narrative, for it emphasises that the order has now come into existence, unlike on the occasion when the two merchants Tapussa and Bhallika were admitted as the very first lay disciples. The Buddha realised that Yasa's father was now freed from 'the cankers', namely sense-pleasures, further existence and ignorance, and that Yasa's own prospects were therefore also good. He therefore let the father see him. True to his position the father told Yasa of his mother's distress and besought him to return, but Yasa looked towards the Buddha who spoke earnestly of Yasa's progress and urged that it would be quite unsuitable for him now to return to the household life. Yasa's father acquiesced and invited the Buddha to come and take a meal with Yasa as his attendant. When the householder had departed with the news, Yasa was ordained as a monk with the appropriate formula. Since Yasa had attained his deliverance during the Buddha's instruction this meant that there were now seven people to whom the title of arahant or 'perfected one' could be applied.

This event was seen as the starting point of an ever-widening circle. The mother and the former wife of Yasa, who entertained the Buddha to a meal, were accepted as the first women lay disciples. Then four other young men of merchant houses in Benares followed Yasa's example: making eleven arahants. After that another fifty followed suit, making a total of sixty-one arahants. All the newly ordained converts marked this step in a uniform way by shaving their hair and beards, putting on yellowish robes and abandoning their homes.

'Fifty' is a round number, and the story of Yasa has other

legendary characteristics. However it seems quite likely that the Buddha's first extensive following should be drawn from merchant families in nearby Benares, attracted by the confident sense of discovery radiated by the initial group under the leadership of the Buddha himself. Yasa's renunciation of the world, stealing out at dead of night and aided in his stealth by the invisible devas, is told in a form which also came to be used for the story of the Buddha's own departure for the forest (see Part Four).

We have to recognise stereotyped legendary models in these stories, rather than direct reporting of historical fact. Yet there was indeed a beginning to the 'going forth' of Buddhist monks, from ordinary life, setting a pattern which has in its essentials been carried on down to the present day.

Ordinations at Uruvela and Rajagaha

We may suppose the beginnings of Buddhism to have been informal, almost accidental. Still, it seems that the Buddha was personally responsible for initiating a more structured pattern of teaching and discipleship. The monks were sent out alone with instructions to teach the Dhamma, 'lovely at the beginning, lovely in the middle and lovely at the end', for the sake of others who without hearing it would get nowhere, but who on hearing it might make progress. This led to such a coming and going that monks and new candidates alike were worn out on their journeys for ordination purposes. The Buddha therefore sanctioned ordinations by the monks themselves which should be carried out along a defined pattern. Firstly the candidate should be shaven, and he should put on yellow robes with an upper robe over one shoulder. Then he should pay respect at the feet of the monks, squat down and extend his hands with palms together in salute. In this position he repeats the three refuges three times over, and is thereby accepted into the community.

With these arrangements made, and after one rainy season was over, the Buddha set out from Benares to Uruvela. The narrative includes a tale which illustrates the attraction of the Buddha's confidence in his own teaching. On the way he turned aside into a woodland grove to sit in meditation at the root of a tree, when suddenly he was approached by some thirty young men who said they were looking for a woman. They had been having a party in the woods with their wives; except that one of them was unmarried and for him they brought along a woman 'of low standing'. Apparently she had viewed the party from a perspective of her own, for in the course of the merriment she slipped away with some of their belongings. The Buddha challenged them to stop looking for the woman and instead to seek their true selves (a looser use of the word *atta* than in the teaching about *anatta* given earlier). They sat down and were persuaded to such an extent that they were ordained on the spot. This story is a lively and brief addition to the account of the Buddha's impact on others.

The next by contrast is long and repetitive, dealing with a more or less professional contest at Uruvela between the Buddha and three religious leaders all named Kassapa. Each of these was the chief of a band of ascetics who wore matted hair, performed sacrifices, tended sacred fires and dived into cold river waters in mid-winter. There is obviously reminiscence here of another set of religious specialists on the banks of the river Neranjara. The holy men of ancient India were supposed to have supernatural powers of various kinds, such as the powers of mind-reading, swift and invisible travel, psychic projection and psychic control of physical phenomena. It is in these terms that the Buddha's encounter with the overall leader of all these ascetics, Kassapa of Uruvela, is couched. He performed feat after feat to demonstrate his psychic superiority and eventually suggested to Kassapa that he was not yet an arahant, nor even on the way to becoming one. Kassapa finally gave in and received ordination, whereupon hundreds of others followed suit, cutting off their matted hair and abandoning their fire-worshipping accessories.

This story is historically interesting for two reasons. Firstly it illustrates yet again the existence of a varied religious community in the forest, trying various techniques of spiritual satisfaction, but ready to recognise the clear personal authority of the Buddha. Secondly, it suggests again that the Buddha's initial encounter with others was first set in the language which they themselves used. Thus his first display of psychic power was to demonstrate his fearlessness of the sacred fire maintained by Kassapa, by staying next to it overnight in meditation and 'mastering heat by heat'.

Feats such as these, many involving the use of fire and thus geared to the interests of the matted hair ascetics, eventually provided the occasion for explaining the Dhamma. When all had been ordained he preached a sermon on 'burning'. In effect this is a meditation on the six senses, that is, the five ordinary senses plus the mind, and all the things which they mediate to us. All of these are burning with passion, hatred and stupidity, and they burn because of birth, age, death and suffering. For this reason a monk should disregard each of these, the eye, visible shapes, the ear and audible sounds, and so on. Through this disregarding or 'dispassion' the monk will be freed and no longer subject to rebirth.

Two more important ordinations are recorded as taking place at Rajagaha, where the Buddha next resided. These were the famous disciples Sariputta and Moggallana. Yet again the story illustrates the way in which the Buddha's teaching arose among competing doctrines and drew followers from rival groups. Both Sariputta and Moggallana lived the homeless life among a group of 250 men under the leadership of Sanjaya, apparently without being convinced that the latter had fully solved the spiritual problems which exercised them all. The two made an agreement that whichever of them should be the first to attain 'the deathless' should tell the other. It so happened that the monk Assaji, who was one of the original five companions of the Buddha, came into the town of Rajagaha to collect alms. Sariputta caught sight of him and was so impressed by his pleasant deportment and clear expression that he wanted to know who his teacher was. He waited until Assaji had finished his round of alms-collecting, then greeted him and asked him that very question.

Assaji replied that his teacher was a member of the Sakya people, but that as he himself was only recently instructed he could only give a brief idea of what the teaching was. Sariputta insisted that he did not need a long account, so Assaji explained that the Buddha taught of the cause of those things which have a cause, and also of their 'stopping'. Sariputta thereupon himself saw the point of this teaching, saying that it reached 'as far as the sorrowless path', which had been unknown for millions of years. He returned to his friend Moggallana who in turn was impressed by his clear complexion. Sariputta explained how he had 'attained the deathless' with the result that Moggallana too was convinced. They both went off to report to their 250 companions who all agreed to go with them to seek ordination under the Buddha. Only the leader, Sanjaya, was displeased, and he tried to prevent their departure by offering to share his leadership of the group with the other two. This was to no avail, even though he asked them the proverbial three times. Sariputta and Moggallana went off with the others, leaving Sanjaya spitting hot blood. The two new disciples were well received by the Buddha who gave them a position of leadership within the Samgha.

As to the historicity of this story in its particular detail, there is little that can be said either way. In the *Mahavagga* the legend is relatively simple and unembroidered. By contrast, plenty of detail was added in later writings, not least about the position of seniority awarded to the two monks which may reflect contemporary or later rivalries. On the other hand even this simple story is made up of stylised elements which were the natural means of passing on any tradition at all, but which therefore partake to some extent of artificiality.

Succcess and opposition

In retelling the narrative leading on from the Buddha's enlightenment, a number of short cuts have been taken above, mainly to overcome the repetitions of stylised phraseology which many modern readers find irksome. But one story, which brings out a whole new aspect of the emergent religion, occurs in the *Mahavagga* between the ordination legends. This is the story of the Buddha's encounter with King Bimbisara.

Initially, it should be remembered, the Buddha had been a lonely, wandering hermit who had completely renounced household life and worldly interests. With the legend of his meeting with Bimbisara his personal discovery was brought right to the centre of political power at the time. Bimbisara was the king of Magadha referred to above in Chapter Two, and he resided at Rajagaha, where the Buddha had now arrived. The story is told with much circumstance but, let us admit it, little drama, for the king heard of the Buddha's reputation, came to greet him and to hear him, and was persuaded. There were many Brahmans present (were there really 120,000?) and also many householders. One of the sidelights is that the crowd saw Kassapa of Uruvela arrive and they wondered whether the Buddha followed him or vice versa. Since the Buddha knew what was in their minds he asked Kassapa why he had abandoned the sacred fire, and Kassapa replied publicly that he had done so in order to become the Buddha's disciple. With this made clear to all, the Buddha expounded his teaching, Bimbisara recognised it, and was accepted as a lay-disciple. The king also announced that while his first ambition in life had been to be anointed monarch, his other ambitions had been to have the Buddha come into his kingdom, to pay homage to him, to be taught by him and to understand his teaching. These other ambitions were now all realised. The king thereupon invited the Buddha and his fellow monks to a meal the next day, and on that occasion presented the company with a bamboo grove which was both secluded and conveniently placed, where they might stay.

These acts of patronage are very important, for they symbolise the sure historical fact that the Buddha's teaching and the monastic order that went with it quickly achieved social recognition at the highest level. What had begun as the intensely personal cult of a few individual hermits quickly achieved a social reality which in one way or another the Buddhist religion has maintained in some countries if not in others. Bimbisara's 'ambitions' indicate a twinning of the concepts of 'king' and 'buddha' which were often to be linked thereafter, though of course Bimbisara's speech as given in the narrative itself is sure to be a secondary concoction and so we must reckon with some retrospective 'reading in'. However that may be, there is no doubt that the Buddha did address himself to the highest levels of political and social life, as well as to the lowest, and this remained a definite feature of the religion which he founded.

If the conversion of King Bimbisara seemed breathtakingly easy the progress of the order was not entirely without obstacle. The very last piece of this extended narrative registers complaints about the young men streaming out of the respectable families of Magadha to join the Buddha's order. People grumbled at being left without their sons, and wives grumbled at being left as *de facto* widows. Quite apart from the conversion of matted hair ascetics and other wanderers, who presumably did not function in any case as pillars of ordinary society, the Buddha was now effectively breaking up family life. The Buddha seems to have been unperturbed by these noises. The narrative quaintly gives out his prediction that it would last for seven days and then stop, which not surprisingly turns out to come true. Of greater interest is perhaps the argument which the disciples were instructed to give in reply to any such complaints. This was simply that Buddhas led people by 'true Dhamma', and therefore one could have no grounds for jealousy or regret if people went out and followed it. This was indeed a self-confident answer, one may observe, and one which underlines the basic assumption of the Buddha's teaching that it was those who left the household life, elsewhere regularly described as 'full of hindrances', who might hope to attain the highest goal. The order presupposed 'going forth', and it also presupposed the continued existence of a respectful laity to provide alms. Apparently, since the hubbub died away, there was sufficient positive faith within the food and wealth producing classes to support the new religious order.

If we draw together the threads of monarchy, monks and people it is easy to see that a three-cornered relationship had been struck in which all played mutually supporting roles. This may be presented diagrammatically as follows (K for king, P for people, and S for Samgha, the monastic community):

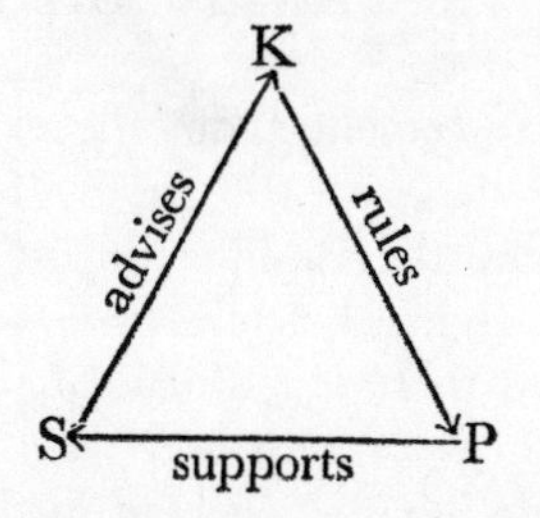

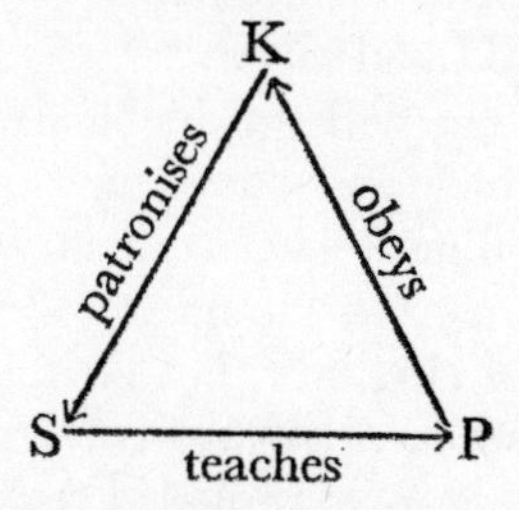

These diagrams take account of the ancient Buddhist view of the *cakkavatti or* 'wheel-turning' monarch, who just as the Buddha turns the wheel of Dhamma, rolls out his own royal wheel of benevolent dominion in all quarters, after being advised on moral law by the monks. Such a coexistence between the three estates was surely adumbrated in the Buddha's own time through acts of patronage, though it found its full flowering at the time of Asoka and in later Buddhist kingdoms elsewhere.

The discipline

With the Buddha's answer to complaints from respectable families the narrative section of the discipline books comes to a halt. We have seen a concentration on the Buddha's own enlightenment forming the centre-piece of a cluster of texts, containing various well-known summaries of his teaching, and in the case of the *Mahavagga* running out into a series of tales about the establishment of the order. Now whatever may be the historical value of any one or two of the particular details given above, this whole cluster of narratives in the corporate Buddhist memory is one of the most important funnels of tradition through which we may peer back into what actually happened in those early days.

But from that point on the discipline texts form a timeless miscellany. There are more stories within the texts, but they are scattered about. The most prominent feature is the endless variety of rules about food and clothing and other aspects of the monks' daily life. Suffice it here to mention the ten rules given to new monks, which have retained a central place in Buddhist discipline ever since. They run as follows: no taking of life, no stealing, no sexual intercourse, no lying, no intoxication, no eating at the wrong time, no show of dancing or music, no decorations and ointments on the body, no sleeping on raised beds, no acceptance of gold and silver.

There will no doubt always be disagreement about the extent to which the many questions referred to in all the pages of the discipline books were in fact settled by the Buddha during his lifetime. On the one hand the sheer weight of detail seems to be out of character, but on the other hand there is a streak of pragmatism which rings true, allowing concessions to meet particular circumstances provided that the ultimate intention is held in sight. Just one encounter of particular interest may be related, for it modifies the strong stance taken by the Buddha when families objected to their sons leaving home. It also brings in persons related to the Buddha personally, though of course it must be stressed that this does not really give historical certainty about these relationships.

After staying in Rajagaha the Buddha travelled to Kapilavatthu (Sanskrit, Kapilavastu), and went to visit the home of his own family. Two are named, his father, Suddhodana, and his son, Rahula. Rahula's mother, who is not named, told her son to go to his father and ask for his inheritance. He did so, but the Buddha stepped away from him. When he asked again the Buddha told Sariputta to ordain him, which he did, according to the formula explained earlier. Suddhodana then approached the Buddha himself, and said that he had a petition. The Buddha was again brusque, saying that it was not his business to grant petitions. Suddhodana tried again, and this time being given permission to put his request, he said that just as the Buddha's own departure had caused great sorrow, so had that of Nanda, elsewhere named as the Buddha's half-brother, and now so too did the 'going forth' of Rahula. A parent's love for a son cuts right through to the marrow in the bone, he argued, and therefore it would be good if ordinations were to take place only with parental consent. Upon this the Buddha gave a talk about his teaching which satisfied Suddhodana well, and then he declared that it would henceforth be an offence to ordain without parental consent. Quite apart from the possible biographical value of this brief nugget of tradition (and it is told simply enough to ring true), it exemplifies clearly the way in which new rules were invented to regulate ever more satisfactorily the relations between the monks and the people.

PART THREE

NIRVANA

7

Politics, Monks and Householders

Preliminaries

The second of the two great focal points of narrative tradition about the Buddha is his decease or nirvana. Just as with the Buddha's enlightenment, this great event was both a personal model for all his followers and also the starting point of the Buddhist religion in various important ways.

In general it may be said that the Buddhist discipline and teaching were recited and passed on in a variety of different forms which we no longer use for communication today. For example many things were arranged by number, or put into verses. These quickly attain a timeless quality which makes them difficult to evaluate historically, or even to correlate with each other. It was not until long after that various incidents in the Buddha's life were assigned to different times over a period of twenty years. This chronology, though generally accepted to be completely spurious, has nevertheless often been followed by modern writers, and even appears, in a curiously ambivalent form, in Thomas's *The Life of the Buddha.* We must accept that it is just not possible to put together a coherent narrative about the no doubt numerous wanderings of the Buddha. Given the generally miscellaneous character of Buddhist writings, it is therefore particularly striking that narrative did begin to accumulate about the events immediately preceding the Buddha's death. Moreover this narrative, like the story of the enlightenment, was carried forward in various schools of Buddhism, and for all the embroidering which it contains it is therefore part of the basic stock of Buddhist tradition.

Before going into detail, the historical position must be made clear. Some investigators have stressed the work's early character and some have argued that it is late. It must be admitted that it contains many elements which represent a mythologisation of the Buddha. For example, in a discussion of the causes of an earthquake we find a preliminary outline of the fully developed legend of a Buddha's life-story, beginning with his conscious and intentional incarnation from a heavenly realm into his mother's womb. The text is therefore not early in the sense that it altogether predates such ideas, which we have undertaken here to hold over until Part Four below. Nor is the miraculous aspect of legend lacking. Indeed it is rather more prominent than in the enlightenment stories, in which it was more or less possible for it to be overlooked. But even here we shall take only light note of it, for the miraculous element too really belongs to that overall mythologising tendency which we examine later.

What the narrative contains is in fact a museum of all the things about the last days of the Buddha which interested his followers afterwards. Just as with the enlightenment, there is no exact record of his deeds and words. Some of the memories are piously elaborated, some illustrate the practices and problems of a new religious community. However, there is a crucial difference between this narrative and the narratives about the Buddha's birth and infancy. The latter were invented to glorify presumed events. The narrative of the nirvana by contrast was based on a truly remembered event.

It is easy to see that the narrative has grown with time. This is clear from the existence of several ancient editions in Pali, Sanskrit, Chinese and Tibetan, which have all been carefully compared in a detailed study by the German scholar Ernst Waldschmidt (see Note on Sources for details). His work was not available to many earlier writers on the Buddha, whose opinions therefore diverged widely. Detailed commentary is avoided below, but Waldschmidt's work has shown that various stages can be discerned in the development of the text. The very fact that nearly three-quarters of it is found in most ancient editions, but that the remainder is only weakly attested proves this point in principle. It is no longer possible to put a date to any of the sections which are common to all editions. Nor do the sections common to all editions escape legendary heightening. When the Buddha is said to cross the river Ganges miraculously, for example, without any kind of boat, not one edition fails to give the story. On the other hand most sections are certainly the developed form of communal reminiscences which eventually reach right back to the time of the Buddha himself. It is clear that in this fundamental sense the story of the nirvana is a striking complement to the story of the enlightenment.

Political advice

The story of the nirvana begins with the power-hungry Ajatasattu as king of Magadha. It is sufficient indication of his character that he had murdered his own father Bimbisara to take the throne. Now he planned a vicious and unprovoked attack on the neighbouring Vajjian people, threatening to bring them to 'utter ruin'. His chief henchman, for they were little more than dictatorial gangsters, was a Brahman named Vassakara, and he was told to go and seek out the Buddha to get a prediction about the outcome of such an attack.

If there is anything which the Buddha was not, it was court soothsayer. Nor was he a sycophant. It is perhaps surprising therefore that the king thought his advice should be sought about a war of aggression, catering to instincts clearly contrary to the Buddha's own message. The king believed that at any rate 'the Buddhas' do not tell untruths and that they have access to secrets of life unknown to others. He was pragmatist enough to want to hear Vassakara's report, even though it might be unfavourable.

Vassakara set out from the king's city, Rajagaha, in a luxurious carriage, and drove to Vulture Peak, a hill where the Buddha was often to be found. When the carriage could go no farther because of the rough terrain, he went the rest of the way on foot. Finally he arrived at the secluded spot where the Buddha was staying, greeted him with the usual courtesies, and as the king had instructed him, he enquired solicitiously after the Buddha's health. Then he put the king's enquiry about the extent to which the Vajjians might successfully resist attack.

We now come across an example of the way in which the ancient editions vary, for in the Sanskrit and Chinese cases the Buddha replies to Vassakara directly, and then speaks to his disciple Ananda so that the Brahman can overhear, while in the Pali edition it is the other way round. Not all textual variations of this kind will be reported below, so that readers who follow up the English translation of the Pali edition for themselves should not be surprised at minor discrepancies.

The Buddha's reply consisted of recalling a visit which he had made not long before to Vesali, the Vajjian capital, in order to pass the rainy season. (This visit is also attested separately in another sutra.) While there he had taught the Vajjians, who had a republican form of government, seven conditions of social and political welfare. These included regular attendance at their assemblies, agreement on matters of policy, respect for tradition and law, avoidance of sexual immorality, respect for the elders and leaders, maintenance of community religious rites, and giving a friendly and protective reception to arahants. It is evident that these add up to the kind of social legitimation of the state and the Buddhist religion referred to in the previous chapter, only this time in a republican context. The Buddha catechised his disciple Ananda about whether the Vajjians were holding to these principles, one by one, and received each time the answer that they were. In each case the Buddha responded that as long as they did so they might be expected to prosper as a people.

Vassakara listened in to this lengthy rehearsal of the steadfast qualities of the Vajjians, and gradually realised what it meant for the king's enquiry. When it was over he observed that if any one of these conditions was sufficient to ensure the Vajjians' stability, and yet they observed them all, it would be quite impossible for Ajatasattu to overcome them. The Buddha allowed him to draw this conclusion for himself, apparently not deigning to be concerned over much about Ajatasattu's ambitions. Vassakara however seemed to be satisfied that he had received a reliable and useful answer, and he left to attend to all his other urgent political business.

The story of this advice was not included as an idle anecdote. What follows is significant, for it relates the teaching on political stability to the order of Buddhist monks itself. When Vassakara had gone off to report to the king, the Buddha told his chief attendant Ananda to assemble all the other monks together. When this was done the Buddha addressed them on the conditions for the well-being of the community. Firstly these were stated in a form quite analogous to the seven conditions of political well-being. This indeed implies a 'republican' approach to community government, for the first two principles were regular attendance at the formal meetings and general consent about the community's pattern of life. The other conditions follow on: previously agreed regulations should be respected, and the older monks should also be respected and their words well noted. Two of the conditions were modified to relate to monastic life. The prohibition of sexual immorality was generalised, since sexual intercourse of any kind was forbidden to the monks anyway. This was transformed into an injunction not to succumb to craving in any form, for it led to renewed existence. Secondly the maintenance of religious rites for the community was restated as putting a high value on solitary meditation. Finally, the provision of a good reception for monks was applied to mutual hospitality between the different groups of monks.

This reinterpretation of the seven conditions of prosperous social welfare is of interest for two reasons. For one thing it indicates the practical social understanding so characteristic of early Buddhism, which undoubtedly owed a great deal to the personality and manner of its historical founder. Secondly it shows clearly how the Buddhist order and ordinary society were expected to live side by side, reflecting each other in various ways but also allowing a real divergence of role. Householders with a respect for Buddhism might lead healthy lives in accordance with natural morality. This did not contradict the possibility that their children might one day become monks, abstaining from all forms of sensual attachment and particularly that which leads to procreation. Similarly the monks had an interest in seeing a stable society as a basis for undisturbed monastic life. Hence, while they themselves were religious specialists of a certain kind, it was quite acceptable for society in general to cultivate those religious rites, whatever they might be, which acted as its cement.

At this point in the narrative, the fascination of numbers takes over. The compilers were not satisfied with one list of seven conditions for a stable monastic order. There follow another six such lists (five in the Pali), giving a broad variety of modest and earnest qualities which the monks should cultivate. These have nothing much to do with the seven conditions of well-being enjoined upon the Vajjians, except that it is said again and again that if the qualities are observed the monastic community will not decline, but prosper. Since several of the formulae also appear in the *Auguttara-nikaya* (where the Buddha's teaching is given along purely numerical lines) it is clear that standard materials have been brought in here under the heading of 'seven'. The last is a list of six only, but it is related by content, for it refers to the way in which the monks should care for each other, sharing their alms in common, and maintaining that right understanding which leads to the reduction of suffering.

Travels and teachings

It is quite probable that the Buddha gave much other teaching while he stayed at Rajagaha, but we can only presume that it was along the lines of his teaching as otherwise known to us. The Pali edition adds a short sermon at this point, in which the Buddha praised the value of moral conduct, of meditation, and of insight (sometimes called wisdom). These three (*sila, samadhi* and *panna*) are yet another traditional summary of the Buddhist religion. They show that the teaching of the Buddha was construed not as being merely ethical, nor merely yogic, nor merely intellectual, but a combination of all three. The fruit of these three were said to be freedom from the 'cankers', familiar to the reader from the story of the enlightenment. The only difference is that here, as well as sense-pleasures, coming into being and ignorance, is added a fourth canker, namely delusion.

The main outline of the narrative as it develops is that the Buddha left the royal city of Rajagaha and travelled through various places in Magadha, until eventually he crossed the River Ganges into Vajjian territory and spent some time in their capital of Vesali. The editions do not agree entirely about what he taught in each place, but there is certainly general agreement about his move across to the rival capital, in considerable state, giving instruction as he went.

One of the places at which he halted was called Ambalatthika, where he stayed in some kind of royal lodge and repeated the sermon mentioned just above. Or was it perhaps a discourse on the four noble truths which he gave here, as the Sanskrit text records? According to the Pali tradition the talk on the four noble truths was given later at Kotigama, where the Buddha however also repeated yet again the other sermon on morality, meditation and insight. In the meantime he is supposed to have given the very same at Nalanda, and soon after it is recorded once more for his stay at Nadika in the land of the Vajjians. It is clear that no matter whose the territory might be in which he found himself, the basic teaching remained constant.

The teaching on the four noble truths is given in a simple form, entirely consistent with its appearance in the enlightenment story. First comes the truth of suffering, or sorrow (*dukkha*), then the cause of suffering, then the cessation of suffering, and lastly the path which leads to that cessation. The Buddha taught that both he and his fellow-wanderers had travelled so far through the round of birth and rebirth because they had not recognised these truths. If the truths were understood then craving for another existence could be rooted out and there would be no need for yet another rebirth. This simple, more or less classic statement of the teaching inevitably suggests to us that the Buddha himself had attained such a state. His release from the cycle of birth and death is assured, and therefore when his life comes to a close it will be a very special kind of event.

Still in the country of Magadha, we may quickly pass over a talk to Sariputta, found only in the Pali text, referring to the Buddha's position among other Buddhas, past and future. More important are some events at Pataligama (Sanskrit: Pataliputra), just on the Magadhan side of the Ganges. Here the Buddha addressed a mixed gathering of monks and lay disciples. The teaching itself was addressed to the lay disciples as householders, and gives some idea of how the new religion was understood at a popular level. The teaching is given in terms of the disadvantages of living wrongly or carelessly and the advantages of living correctly. A man who lives badly will become poor on account of his indolence, he will get a bad reputation, he will not be able to enter the company of others confidently, he will be in a state of anxiety at death, and he will be reborn somewhere in the hells. If a man lives well on the other hand he will be prosperous, enjoy a good reputation, be confident among others, die without remorse and be reborn in the heavens among the devas (angel-like gods). These diverse prospects spell out what may be called the proximate goal of a blessed rebirth as compared with the eventual Buddhist goal of nirvana.

The talk went on until late at night, and the householders invited the Buddha to stay in their guest-house. Or did the whole scene take place in the guest-house, as the Pali edition describes?

Pataligama was also the site of a fortress being built by the Magadhans to keep out the Vajjians. The Buddha praised the state official in charge, none other than the Vassakara who figured in the opening story, for his selection of the spot. (Additional references to an official named Sunidha may be the result of a misunderstanding in the tradition.) The Buddha himself had perceived protective deities to be present in large numbers, it was said, and on that basis predicted a strong future for the town which would be subject however to three hazards, namely fire, water and internal dissension. After being given a special repast of sweet rice and cakes by Vassakara some verses were uttered by the Buddha. These sanctioned the transfer of the merit which accrued because of the meal to the account of the protective deities, so that in return they would exert themselves on behalf of the newly fortified locality. The Sanskrit edition adds that Vassakara ceremoniously enacted this transfer by a libation of water from a special vessel. This story may be simply reading back into history a desired connection between the town in question and the person of the Buddha. During his lifetime the town was not the Pataliputra (Sanskrit) which it later became, although there seems no reason to doubt that there was a village which the Magadhans fortified at that time. The story is also evidence, not easily denied, for the Buddha's own acceptance of the *de facto* reality of local gods or spirits which were connected with the well-being of their particular places or communities. It will be recalled that one of the good qualities of the Vajjians was said to be their maintenance of proper community rites. One might also conclude that the Buddha respected the integrity of all healthy communities, a diplomatic attitude since he was in a sensitive border area.

The political advice which the Buddha gave seems to have been of a very general character and not particularly partisan or critical. According to some texts the powerful men on both sides of the Ganges all sought to arrange his crossing of the river, which was in full flood. The Buddha's impartiality may have been the starting point of the miracle story of his crossing without any visible means of transport at all. A verse or more are added to give a spiritual meaning. This contrasts the efforts of the ordinary people using boats and rafts with the sovereign freedom of the Buddha to cross the ocean of suffering. But the texts are complicated and the question is vexed.

These opening parts of the story of the nirvana range very widely. However, they show the Buddha respected and followed, giving his basic teaching again and again, and relating it to different groups of people – politicians, householders and monks. The above represents about one sixth of the whole story, and the next two sixths see the Buddha active in Vesali, where the first intimations of his impending decease are heard. The story still maintains a broadly flowing course however, containing various incidents which somehow came to be carried along within it. One thing is beyond doubt. The scene shifted to the capital of the Vajjians.

8

The Buddha's Death Predicted

Future lives

On the other side of the Ganges the Buddha gave the same fundamental teaching as before, though the texts diverge over which sermons were given where. They come to agreement again over a sojourn of the Buddha at Nadika, on the way to Vesali; not indeed about the Pali text's favourite sermon on morality, meditation and insight mentioned earlier and repeated here, but about a longer discussion on existence after death.

The monks have heard on their alms round that a large number of people including the Buddha's own followers have died from an epidemic. Ananda therefore asks the Buddha what their destiny will be, that is, under what circumstances they will be reborn. It is interesting that the Buddha obliged with predictions about them all, indicating the stage which each had reached in the religious life. A monk named Salha, for example, had destroyed the cankers and attained the state of being an arahant, no longer subject to rebirth. A nun is also named, for the Buddha had reluctantly allowed a female order to be established, and this nun, Nanda, is declared to have destroyed the fetters which bind people to the world of desires; she would never return to this world but would be reborn in a heavenly, lustless realm. From there she would attain nirvana without further complications here below. A lay disciple named Sudatta had attained the state of 'once-returner', one who would be born once more in this world and would thereupon make his final escape from suffering. Another named Sugata had completely destroyed three fetters, and would be reborn still some times more. However, he would not be born into a state of suffering (that is, as an animal, as a ghost, or in one of the terrible hells) and would never again fall away from his progress towards nirvana. In these last three categories came many others who had died, numbering more than fifty 'never-returners' (who never return to this world of ours), more than ninety 'once-returners' like Sudatta, and more than five hundred 'stream-winners', who could never again slide back from the path of enlightenment. These various destinies are given in the standard terms of early Buddhism, which illustrate that though perfection may not be attainable nevertheless something less than perfection was also considered by the Buddhists to be very worthwhile.

Most people are interested to know what, if anything, is going to happen to them after death. It is, therefore, striking that after giving these predictions, the Buddha comments that death is a natural occurrence for each one of us and that it was rather tiresome for him to be asked about the future destiny of all these people. Fortunately all had been predicted to good future states, of which the least reassuring was human life. Other births were however possible, namely birth as an animal, birth as a 'hungry ghost', condemned to hunt for scraps of food and never to be satisfied, and birth in one of the 'hells' or 'purgatories' where awful punishments for bad deeds were meted out until all the bad karma was used up. Since most people desire above all not to be reborn in states such as these, the Buddha offered a simple remedy summarised as the 'Mirror of Dhamma'. This consisted of having faith or trust in the Buddha, in the Dhamma and in the Samgha. These are the same as the three things in which 'refuge' is taken in the ordination formula; so in that sense the faith for all is reflected in the meaning of monastic ordination, even though not everybody is ordained. Faith in these three, which includes respecting them and honouring them, would ensure that one would not be reborn in one of the 'states of woe' and, therefore, if a person honestly lived in this faith he could predict a satisfactory rebirth for himself.

The Sanskrit edition opens the enunciation of the 'Mirror of Dhamma' with a reference to the formula of Causal Arising, explained above in Chapter three. This is not surprising since the formula has traditionally been related to the successive births of an individual. When painted as a wheel the five or six states of possible rebirth form the central part of the picture while the twelve links of Causal Arising are represented in the outer rim.

The Buddha receives a courtesan

When the Buddha arrived at Vesali itself he took up position in a nearby grove of mango trees belonging to a high-class courtesan named Ambapali (meaning 'mango grower'). Here he exhorted his monks to be mindful and self-possessed at all times, not being swayed by the yearnings or the depressions common among ordinary people. Whatever they were doing, every bodily movement, every swish of their robes and every handling of their bowls, whether they were eating, or relieving themselves, all of their activities were to be carried out in a self-conscious or attentive way. The Sanskrit edition makes out that the Buddha called his monks particularly to concentration because he had seen some women approaching. All the texts give the story of Ambapali's visit, which was an affair of some state. When her carriage could approach no further she went on foot, and on arrival at the mango grove she sat down respectfully and listened to the Buddha's teaching. Finding it edifying, she invited him to dinner and, in the usual formula, the Buddha showed his consent by not saying anything. Before the meal took place the Buddha was also visited by a large company of Licchavis, who were the leading clan in Vesali. They also wished to invite the Buddha to dinner, and regretted having been outplayed by the 'mango girl'. However the Buddha's word was given and so, noble and attentive though the Licchavis were, the Buddha and his company went to have dinner with Ambapali as promised. In the Pali tradition (including another rehearsal of this story in the Mahavagga in the books of discipline), Ambapali presented the Buddha with the mango grove on this occasion, for use by him and his monks. This presentation is not recorded in other editions, however. Other complications in the texts make it difficult to be sure of the details of any such meetings, and it is quite probable that reminiscences not originating in the Buddha's last weeks of life have been caught up into the gradually expanding narrative. This likelihood is reinforced, in that whole stretches of these narratives are also found separately in other parts of the Buddhist scriptures.

The Buddha's first sickness

As the rainy season was coming on the Buddha told his monks to take up residence in some suitable place near Vesali, wherever they had friends or relatives. He himself retired with Ananda to a little place called Beluva. Here he was taken seriously and painfully ill. Just as he had exhorted his monks he himself remained mindful and self-possessed, and though near to death he reflected that he ought first to speak to them all again. By sheer willpower therefore he fought his sickness and after a while it passed away. Talking with Ananda afterwards, his disciple confided how he himself had felt quite weak on seeing the Buddha suffer. His only comfort had been his belief that the Buddha would have to give instructions about the future of the monastic order, and could scarcely die before that was done.

The Buddha rounded on him sharply. Why should that be necessary? He had never concealed any part of his teaching. It was public to all the monks. There was no secret truth still to be revealed. As to leadership, if anybody else thought that he should be the leader, he could give his own instructions. The Buddha himself was not such a leader and therefore had no particular instructions. He was eighty years old, and his body was like a worn-out cart. In future each monk should be his own lamp and his own refuge, and not seek any external support. The Dhamma should be their lamp and their refuge. This meant that they should be mindful and self-possessed at all times.

Sometimes this injunction 'Be lamps to yourselves' is interpreted as a mere individualism in the religious life. However it was closely linked to the idea of Dhamma, which was preserved corporately by the monks, and therefore did not bear an arbitrary meaning. Clearly, a doctrinaire or magical view of authority was rejected in this famous utterance of the Buddha; but on the other hand it links up with the concern shown by the monks in trying to transmit and interpret the Dhamma correctly.

Reflections on length of life

The Buddha remained some time longer at Vesali and is said to have particularly praised the pleasantness of the place, with its various holy places round about. We no longer know what these shrines were, but they were certainly secluded places singled out since pre-Buddhist times, awesome for some reason in archaic folk-memory, probably with their own guardian spirits. At one such place the Buddha began to speak again to Ananda about the length of life. As a spiritual expert he had attained supernormal facilities, including the power to control and direct the appearance of his body as he desired. Thus, if he wanted to, he would be able to remain in his present state of existence more or less indefinitely, at least as long as the remainder of the world-age in which we find ourselves. Or perhaps this meant at least as long as the hundred years presumed to be naturally allotted.

Ananda was expected to request the Buddha to prolong his life artificially, for the benefit of all his fellow men, but failed to do so. Even when the Buddha repeated himself for a second and third time, Ananda failed to respond. The Buddha thereupon sent him away and thought things over alone.

In these narratives a distinct role is played by the evil tempter, Mara. The text says that Mara came and stood beside the Buddha and spoke to him. This is picture language. Essentially Mara is the tempter within. Ananda's failure to request the Buddha to extend his life is put down to the influence of Mara on his mind. At the same time Buddhist narratives also describe him as an external form, with a voice. So it is that Mara now took Ananda's place and directly urged the Buddha to let his life end forthwith. The Buddha himself had said that his body was worn out and was ready to pass away. So he reflected in his own mind. Mara insisted that all the various followers were now well trained, monks, nuns, male lay disciples and female lay disciples. (These are the four types of followers usually mentioned in Buddhist texts.) They knew the doctrine and were correct in their way of life. Not only that, they were able to explain it all thoroughly to others. The Buddha could therefore pass away at this natural time. Had he not sworn, at the time of the Enlightenment, that he would only pass away when the teaching had become widespread and well established? Now this had come to be, and so he could peacefully die. These were the thoughts of the tempter. On the other side no thoughts are recorded. There is simply the conclusion, which really seems to be a compromise. The Buddha asserted that he would live for three months longer, and with this Mara had to be satisfied.

There is of course no suggestion that the Buddha in any way gave in to Mara's temptings. Had he done so it would have implied a readiness to give up life immediately. To say to Mara that he could be content with learning that the Buddha would die in three months, was just a rhetorical brush-off, like contemptuously showing a meatless bone to a dog. The three months was a deliberate judgement on the part of the Buddha himself about the time needed to give his followers some final teaching and prepare for his departure. On one hand it was a conscious prolongation, against the stirrings of Mara-inspired thoughts, and on the other hand it was a shortening of the full hundred years to which he could have extended himself had he chosen. The decision is celebrated in the narrative by an earthquake, so portentous was the occasion deemed to be; and the earthquake is followed by an account of all the times in a Buddha's life when earthquakes happen. This gives a stylised view of a Buddha's total life story to which we shall return in the last stage of development below. But the passage diverts the flow of the story, which really only brings in one earthquake to magnify the Buddha's great resolve. Not content with explaining the eight causes of earthquake, the Pali edition further confuses the story by eight types of assembly in which the Buddha was able to appear to give teaching; eight levels of mastery over sense-perceptions (so that one is not deluded by them), and eight stages of deliverance from the worlds of form and ideas. Presumably these were all included here because of the number eight.

If we pursue the story without being led astray by interruptions we find that the Buddha next reported his experience to Ananda. First he told him how he had been tempted just after his enlightenment to pass away immediately into nirvana. Now Mara had appeared to him again to make him cut short his active life of teaching, and he had settled for just three months more. Ananda was not surprisingly most upset at this, and now he began to beg the Buddha to prolong his life. Three times he requested him but three times he was refused. The chance of making that request had passed. Ananda had missed his opportunity. Just to rub it in, the narrative then shows the Buddha recalling other times and places, for example Vulture Peak and also the Banyan Grove, both near Rajagaha, as well as many others, where he had told Ananda how he had the power to prolong his life indefinitely. Alas, Ananda had never besought him to do so. The matter is then linked to fundamental Buddhist teaching. Whatever is dear to us is sure one day to be separated from us. Whatever comes into being is sure to be dissolved. Similarly the Buddha's life has to come to its ending, and once the decision about this time has been taken it cannot be changed again.

All these reflections on the length of the Buddha's life are clearly an elaborated story based on the attitude towards death which his disciples remembered him to have displayed. They are acted out through the conversations with Ananda and Mara. In sum, they add up to a picture of a man who knew that his life's work was done, and satisfactorily done, and who for himself was attached neither to life nor to death. Neither Ananda's failure to get him to prolong his life, nor Mara's urgent temptation to end it, dislodged him from his dispassionate interest in the well-being of his community, and his readiness to pass away altogether at the appropriate time. This must be how he was historically remembered.

To his monks he therefore now returned. Ananda was told to gather together all the monks living near Vesali and to assemble them in a hall which they had at their disposal, known as the Kutagara Hall. There the Buddha sat down on a mat and addressed them all. The order of his address is no longer agreed, but in short he reminded them of his teaching and announced his forthcoming departure. We do not know whether the Buddha himself really used itemised forms of teaching, such as 'four meditations', 'five moral powers', the 'eightfold path'. Even if he did, there must be many numbered formulae in the canonical writings which were devised after his death. However the main point here is that the Buddha recalled the salient points of his teaching to them all. In particular he reminded them that all compounded things are transient and therefore he enjoined them all, to use the famous phrase, 'Strive diligently!'

The final nirvana of the Buddha was but three months away.

9

The Buddha's Last Journey

From Vesali to Pava

After his first illness the Buddha travelled about another hundred miles before arriving at his final resting place, from Vesali in the territory of the Vajjians, to Kusinara in the land of the Mallas to the north-west. We do not know what motive he had for undertaking this journey, and indeed in historical reality he may have had some further destination in mind, or indeed no particular destination. The tradition is strong however that early one morning he gathered alms in Vesali, ate his meal and returned to the forest just beyond. As he left the town he turned himself round full square towards the city and looked at it for the last time. This look of farewell was called an 'elephant's look', because elephants turn not just their head but their whole body when they turn round to look behind them. Thus the Buddha departed from the city which had been so hospitable to him and took the path into Malla country.

At some point he must have crossed the river Gandaki, a large tributary joining the Ganges some miles above Pataligama (Pataliputra). This itself is not recorded in the narratives, but each edition names a string of villages where the Buddha stayed. The five referred to in the Pali text are Bhandagama, Hatthigama, Ambagama, Jambugama and finally, Bhoganagara. At each place he gave his teaching, recorded now only in stylised form. As such, it falls into two parts. The first part is easily confused with the four noble truths, but actually refers to good conduct, meditation, insight, and release. Each of these is described as 'noble', and when they are realised, it is said to lead to the rooting out of craving and hence of future births. If it sounds like a variation on the four noble truths it also is reminiscent of the three-fold formula of morality, meditation and insight. Indeed with this cue the regular sermon on these three also follows for each of the villages visited. Morality, meditation and insight, it may be recalled, bring release from the cankers of sensuality, coming to be, ignorance and delusion. Some editions also add the previously mentioned account of eight kinds of assembly among whom the Buddha appears to teach, and who rejoice in his teaching because he appears in a form similar to that of his audience. With the variations between the texts and the absence of clear chronology or real knowledge of the places visited, it is clear that narrative history cannot be constructed out of these details. However, all are agreed that on his last journey the Buddha stayed among many people at ordinary places and delivered his teaching in the normal way.

At the last village mentioned, at Bhoganagara, the Buddha gave a different talk of great importance. He was staying at a holy place named after Ananda, presumably a name given much later to honour the famous disciple. This talk may be known as the talk on 'the four great authorities'. Although earlier the Buddha had declared that no particular final instructions were necessary, this talk certainly sounds like such instructions. The question is: how are the monks to know what is orthodox and what is not? It hardly needs to be pointed out that this is a question of great importance to a religion which has just lost its founder. Hence it is not surprising that in their recollection of the Buddha's last days his followers should have found a place for some guidelines in this respect.

Suppose a monk claims to his fellow monks that he knows a teaching which he heard direct from the Buddha's own mouth. How is it to be received? Or supposing a monk reports a teaching which he has heard from another company of monks some distance off, at some place or other; or a monk hears a teaching from the elders of another community, who know the tradition well; or he hears it from a single monk who is thoroughly imbued with the doctrine and the rules? These four are the so-called 'four great authorities'. Yet in fact they are not treated as authoritative sources of Buddhist teaching in themselves. The Buddha goes on to say, and the argument is elaborated separately for each case, that such reports should be received at first with neither praise nor scorn. Every piece of reported teaching should be carefully considered so that its meaning is understood. Then it should be compared with the known teachings, the sutras, and with the known rules, the vinaya. If it does not fit in with these it should be discarded, but if it does fit in it may be accepted as truly representing the word of the Buddha.

In practice therefore the 'four great authorities' turn out to be testable against one great authority, namely tradition remembered through recitation. This is of interest for two reasons. Firstly, although the passage as we have it is undoubtedly late in form, it seems to suggest that there was originally a recognised standard of teaching and discipline which, though relatively brief in itself, formed the basis of the later scripture traditions. This norm, though perhaps never absolutely precisely defined, may well have included a disciplinary code such as that rehearsed at the fortnightly gatherings, and some of the standardised doctrinal formulae such as the four noble truths. We shall never know what the minimal form of this tradition was. Yet it can be presumed to go back eventually to the Buddha himself. Secondly, the passage shows how Buddhist literature came to be developed. If some variant form of a sutra or of some list of doctrines became generally current, it could easily be accepted as part of the orthodox tradition provided that it was consistent with it. Thus countless variants arose. The old materials were repeated in different contexts, new summaries and lists were devised and added to the corporate memory, and explanatory diversions became commonplace. It is not surprising that in some schools the scriptures grew in one shape, while elsewhere they grew differently. Thus the introduction to the discipline books of the Lokottaravadins, namely the *Mahavastu,* contains many stories whose equivalents we find in the sutra section of the Theravadins. What was the Buddha's own personal responsibility for all this? As to details of the development, one must say that it was very little, if any. However he left his religious order with tolerable elasticity while urging the members themselves to weigh up whether new versions of the tradition were consistent in their meaning (not in their letter, incidentally) with all that had gone before.

At Bhoganagara the Buddha added his usual talk on morality, meditation and insight, and then went on with a large escort of monks to another place, and a fateful one, named Pava.

The Buddha's second sickness

At Pava the Buddha took up residence in a grove of trees, where he was visited by a metal-smith named Chunda. Some editions tell us that the grove actually belonged to Chunda, but of course it may simply be that it was linked with his name because of the subsequent events. We are not told what the Buddha taught Chunda – perhaps it was one of his set pieces on four noble truths, or on morality, meditation and insight. Whatever the particular form, he surely told him of suffering as the keynote of existence, and the way to end it by achieving release from the attachments of the senses. As so often, the hearer invited the Buddha and his fellow monks to a meal at his home. In the usual ceremonial way the Buddha accepted the invitation by keeping silent, and Chunda made his exit while keeping his right side turned towards the Buddha.

The text tells us that Chunda went home that night and started cooking. However, we may suppose him to have been a man of some substance and domestic organisation. He was inviting a considerable body of men to eat with him the next day. The menu was two-fold. First he prepared sweet rice and cakes, a standard food of a sort to set before guests. Secondly there was a dish whose identity has been disputed, but which was certainly intended to be considered a special delicacy. Those who think of the Buddha as a vegetarian tend to argue that it was a dish of truffles, or perhaps 'sandalwood mushrooms' as one Chinese translation has it. It seems just as likely however that it was a dish of tenderised pork which Chunda had prepared.

The Buddha arrived next morning, dressed in his robe and bearing his bowl, accompanied by a gathering of monks. When they were all seated he instructed Chunda to give the monks the sweet rice and cakes. The other dish was to be served to the Buddha only. This Chunda did. When they had eaten the Buddha further instructed Chunda that whatever was left over of the truffles, or pork, was to be disposed of by being buried in the ground. This was because there was no one in heaven or earth who could digest it properly except for a Tathagata, that is, a Buddha. This Chunda also did. On his return he came near to the Buddha and once again heard his teaching. The details of this meal are most explicit in the Pali edition, which may indicate that this particular edition did more to bring out the drama of the Buddha's anticipation of his death. Thus, only the Buddha eats the special dish, not because of some privilege, but because it bore his destiny in it. The remainder has to be buried because only a Tathagata can digest it. Even that turns out to be provisional. After the meal the Buddha was seized with a severe attack of dysentery, bringing him near to death. He bore it however without complaint, in a state of 'mindfulness' and 'self-possession'. The sickness passed, and the Buddha set off for Kusinara with Ananda and others.

The road to Kusinara

On the way to Kusinara (Sanskrit: Kusinagara), the Buddha stopped to rest. Some editions tell us that he suffered from pains in his back. Ananda spread out the Buddha's robe, folded into four, and the Buddha lay down. He asked Ananda to fetch water, which he did. But as the river had been muddied by the passage of carts he used it only for washing his feet and his face. This done they went for drinking water to another stream nearby. The Pali edition turns this story into a miracle. The Buddha has to ask Ananda three times to fetch water, while the latter pretends that the river has been muddied by five hundred carts. When Ananda finally goes to the river he finds that it is flowing miraculously clean again. This miraculous heightening is evidence of the later religious consciousness. The historical origin must be that the Buddha had by now become tired on his journeys, and needed refreshment.

The road from Pava to Kusinara was the scene of an encounter with a well-to-do young man named Pukkusa. The Buddha was seated beneath a tree when Pukkusa came along from the opposite direction. He greeted the Buddha and sat down in his company, praising the calmness of mind which the Buddha seemed to display. He may have been a follower of that other holy man

Alara Kalama, one of the well-known spiritual teachers of the time under whom the Buddha himself had once learned. If we are to accept the evidence of the cycle of stories based on the enlightenment, Alara Kalama had died long since. It was by reputation that the young man knew of him. He had heard once how the sage had been seated near the roadside beneath a tree when five hundred carts had passed by. In spite of the noise and the dust, Alara Kalama had noticed not a thing. He had not been asleep, but fully awake and conscious. However his state of mind had been so calm that he had not been affected in any way by the heavy traffic.

The Buddha replied to this feat by recalling a similar performance of his own. The narrative knows no shyness in presenting the Buddha as not wishing to be outdone. His feat was that he had been completely unmoved by a tremendous thunderstorm in which two farmers and four oxen had been killed. A crowd of people had assembled and they could not believe that the Buddha did not know what had been going on. Just like Alara Kalama he had been fully awake and conscious, but his calmness of mind was such that he had been in no way agitated by the thunderstorm, to the extent of simply not noticing that it had taken place. In both these stories conversions had resulted, and so in the same way Pukkusa himself declared himself so impressed by the Buddha's superior achievement that he became a lay disciple on the spot.

Pukkusa wished to mark his new discipleship with a gift and so sent a servant to fetch two robes made of shimmering golden cloth. The Buddha accepted one of these for himself, and one for Ananda. Pukkusa then listened attentively to the Buddha's teaching and finally went his way, leaving the Buddha and Ananda with their new robes. Ananda helped the Buddha to put on the gleaming new garments, but the wonder was that when they were arranged on the Buddha's body they seemed to lose their lustre. Once again this is a miraculous heightening of the story but the dramatic intention lies in the explanation. The Buddha's own body colour was so bright, it is said, that the colour of bright gold lost its sparkle in contrast. This happens on two occasions only. The first is the night during which a Buddha realises his supreme attainment of enlightenment. The second is the night in which he finally passes away, leaving nothing whatever behind, that is, the night of nirvana without residue. With this foreboding the Buddha went on to predict quite specifically that he would die that night, in the third watch, between two sal trees, in a grove near Kusinara.

Although the Buddha's conversations were mainly with his attendant disciple Ananda, he seems to have been accompanied in his final travels by quite a crowd of monks. They went on next to a river named Kakuttha where the Buddha bathed and drank, and from there to a mango wood where he rested again. It is odd that he was attended this time not by Ananda but by another monk named Chundaka. The later commentator Buddhaghosa gives the rather desperate explanation, or rationalisation, that Ananda had stayed behind at the stream to wash out the clothes in which the Buddha had bathed. More likely is some mental association, or confusion, between Chundaka the monk and Chunda the metal-smith. Some verses in the text leave us with a picture of Chunda himself seated before the weary master. Was the monk a relative of Chunda, or was it Chunda himself who had left his smithy to join the order?

The question of the Buddha's illness and impending death was now in everybody's mind. Could it be that it was the special meal prepared by Chunda which was responsible for the Buddha's weak condition? To this matter the Buddha now addressed himself. In fact he spoke to Ananda (who must have returned from doing the washing!), and took the problem in its trickiest form. Who could feel worse than Chunda himself, if by preparing a special meal in the Buddha's honour he had unwittingly brought about his death? There would surely be somebody ready to make him feel thoroughly guilty. If so, Chunda should be told, said the Buddha to Ananda, that he had done well not only to provide the Buddha with food but even to have been the one to have given him his last, fatal meal. He should be told that this was the Buddha's own word, that there were two sorts of offering which far surpassed all others. These were the offering of food to a newly enlightened Buddha, and the offering of food which leads to his final, remainderless nirvana. Therefore Chunda had attained great merit indeed by his offering. His good karma would lead to long life and good fortune, happy rebirths and spiritual advancement.

In this way the Buddha expressly declared that no blame should be attached to Chunda. On the contrary, he was privileged to have played a role in bringing to an end the Buddha's natural life. So saying, the Buddha continued his journey to Kusinara.

The Mallas come to meet the Buddha

The young man Pukkusa, who came towards the Buddha from Kusinara, had belonged to the Malla people. Now the news of his impending arrival had spread and many more people came out from the city to meet him. The Sanskrit edition, though often more restrained, here includes more than the Pali edition. The Mallas decided, it would appear, that his arrival should be turned into a festival. In particular the road leading towards Kusinara was to be cleaned and tidied.

Somewhere in the road lay a huge rock which had blocked it completely, and the advance party of Mallas sent back for reinforcements. All the Mallas thereupon sallied forth from the city bringing horses and camels, bullocks and elephants. Some of them put a rope round the huge rock and tried to drag it away. Others tried to smash it into smaller pieces. Still more tried magical formulae. All was in vain however, and when the Buddha drew near, the rock still lay there just as before.

This rock now became the occasion of the Buddha's teaching to the Mallas. He offered to shift it himself, and thereupon threw it high into the air to fall as dust upon the earth. The Mallas were most impressed at this miraculous feat and requested him to reconvert it into its original form, which he did. The point of this miracle story was to introduce an extended statement of the Buddha's powers. First he had various physical powers which were far beyond those of oxen, yaks, rhinoceroses, elephants, and so on. He also had a tremendous amount of merit, far surpassing that of all the inhabitants of Jambudvipa (i.e. India), and indeed that of billions of gods as well. Added to these were his incomparable power of insight and other supernormal powers. But where is this story leading? The extravagance of the claims made for the Buddha leads the stupefied Mallas to ask whether there is any power which is greater than those already named. The Buddha replies that there is the power of impermanence. All his other powers were about to come to nought that very night together with his own impermanent body. So we see that the whole miraculous extravaganza is designed to be brought at last to the judgement bar of impermanence. The Mallas are upset at the news of the Buddha's impending nirvana. But he shows them once again the rock with which they had struggled so hard. It had finger-marks in it where generations of men in ancient times had practised some kind of physical exercises. Even the great rock was subject to wear and impermanence.

Did this whole story perhaps arise out of a chance occasion when the Buddha used a worn rock to illustrate the ultimately transient character of all things? It is one of the cases where the Sanskrit edition of the text rivals the Pali edition in the insertion of extra materials and a readiness to relate miraculous stories. On the road to Kusinara it was particularly appropriate that such a rock should have been found, tough and immovable, apparently; yet subject as all things, including the Buddha himself, to an eventual passing away without remainder.

10

Between Two Sal Trees

The Buddha lies down

It was not the town of Kusinara itself which the Buddha made his destination, but as usual the woodland just outside. He went with Ananda and other companions to a grove of sal trees. The sal tree is a large tree with hard, dark brown wood, and it grows in groves or spinneys. Here among the trees the Buddha wished to lie down because of his weariness, and a spot was chosen for a low platform or bed which Ananda covered with a cloth or robe. All the texts agree that the position was between two of the sal trees, with the Buddha's head towards the north. This position may have been intended to indicate that the Buddha was not like ordinary men, whose head would be directed to the south in honour of departed ancestors. By contrast, the northerly direction linked the Buddha with the gods. This suggestion is supported by a later indication that the funeral pyre was circumambulated clockwise, with the pyre on the right. This makes it a religious service rather than an ordinary funeral, and hence a sign of the divinisation of the Buddha by his followers, at least at some later date. It is difficult to be certain about the ramified meaning of such details, because so many more small points are now lost to us than were retained. It may simply be that the Buddha pointed his head towards his original home to the north, towards which he had also been travelling. However it is clear that the Buddha adopted a stately posture, reclining on his right side, his left leg lying on top of his right leg, and his head supported by his right hand, the elbow to the ground. This position has been sculptured very frequently, and statues showing it are particularly common in Theravada countries, many of them huge.

The texts provide us with some miracles to complete the tableau.

The sal trees blossomed out of season and scattered their petals over the Buddha. Not content, there came more blossoms out of the sky, then sandalwood powder and finally celestial music. These miracles may remind us that our sources are after all fairly distant from the real scene. The original event has been turned into a painting. Such an opportunity for teaching was not to be missed; and the Buddha points out to Ananda that these decorations are not the right way to honour the Buddha. The right way is to observe the precepts of the Buddhist life.

Mourning is not appropriate

The story is rather haphazardly arranged in the old narratives, but one of the recurrent threads within it is the extreme sadness which fell upon those present. Yet this sadness was said to be misplaced, which leaves a certain tension between the emotions of the people and the meaning of the Buddha's own experience. The matter is introduced in a more or less fanciful way. A monk named Upavana was standing in front of the Buddha to fan him, but the latter asked him to stand aside. Ananda wondered why this service should be so peremptorily rejected. The Buddha's answer was that Upavana had been blocking the view of a vast number of spirit beings who crowded every spot for miles around to see the Buddha during his last hours. These spirits were allegedly grumbling because Upavana was in their way. The anecdote is another of the non-historical extravagances built in to the story as a whole, but its effect is to initiate the theme of mourning. There were some spirits who have celestial status but are worldly at heart, the Buddha continued, and it was these who mourned wildly, hair dishevelled, arms stretched out, weeping loudly, and even rolling on the ground in their despair at the Buddha's passing. There were also spirits on the earth who did the same. But there were other spirits too who were calm in mind. These remembered the teaching that all things which come into being are impermanent and therefore, though reverent, they did not bewail the Buddha's passing away.

It was not long before Ananda himself was overcome with grief. He withdrew to a shelter used by the monks, leaned against the doorway and wept. He thought of his own elementary religious state and of the kindness of his master. How would he be able to manage without him? The Buddha noticed his absence and sent for him to return. When he came back the Buddha told him not to weep, for after all his own teaching was that it is the very nature of things to be impermanent. Every being which came to be, had to be eventually dissolved. Yet Ananda had done well in looking after the Buddha with such care and affection. He should persevere and then he would soon win freedom from the 'cankers'. Ananda had been particularly clever, the Buddha went on, in knowing when to let people come forward to speak with him. Moreover when fellow monks came to visit Ananda himself they would rejoice in his words, and so too would nuns, or lay disciples, male and female. In this he was like a king of kings. Thus comforted and reassured Ananda ceased to mourn.

In another way the good monk Ananda was still dissatisfied. If the Buddha really was about to die, then it should be a matter of great renown bringing benefit to many people, and properly honoured by them all. So he asked the Buddha at least not to die at a little town like Kusinara. It was just an ordinary provincial place in the jungle, a 'wattle-and-daub town' to borrow Rhys Davids' catchy phrase. Kusinara (Sanskrit: Kusinagara) was indeed a small place, identified again in modern times as Kasia, about thirty-four miles (55 km) from Gorakhpur in Uttar Pradesh. Ananda tried to suggest other places where the Buddha might more appropriately die: Savatthi (Sanskrit: Sravasti), Vesali (Vaisali), Rajagaha (Rajagrha), Benares and so on. All of these had many wealthy and aristocratic inhabitants who would honour the Buddha's remains properly. The Buddha rejected Ananda's complaints not as one might expect, on practical grounds or by arguing that a small place would be more fitting. Instead we find the thoroughly Indian argument that Kusinara *used* to be a royal city named Kusavati many miles across and ruled by a great king named Mahasudassana. It had been a prosperous and worldly place filled with elephants, horses and chariots, ringing out with music and the sound of merry feasting. The Buddha then told the story of this great king Mahasudassana.

Interestingly enough this story is given as a separate sutra in the Pali canonical writings, while in the Sanskrit edition it is included within the narrative of the Buddha's last days. According to Waldschmidt the Theravada Buddhists took this very long and elaborate sutra out of its context, but it seems much more likely that it was first a separate piece arising out of the 'wattle-and-daub' taunt, and eventually added on to the main story as in the Pali, or added into it as in the Sanskrit. The sutra also appears as a *jataka* (No. 95), for it deals with a previous existence of the Buddha himself. Mahasudassana had been a great and brilliant monarch who in due course came near to the point of death. The queen and all the court and people wept profusely, but the king restrained them by preaching the doctrine of impermanence. It turns out that this was a previous version of the Buddha's own death. Indeed it was the seventh time that the Buddha had died in that one spot, which was therefore quite appropriate for his final passing away as a Buddha. Not only that, the story picks up the theme of mourning and impermanence already encountered before. To mourn the Buddha who departs is still to be attached to the world. One who understands and accepts his doctrine would not be filled with regrets but would stand by with calm respect.

Ananda was then sent off to Kusinara to inform the Malla people who lived there that the Buddha's death was approaching. The intention of this was to relieve them of any feelings of self-reproach they might have if they failed to visit him through sheer ignorance. Needless to say the Mallas, men, women and children alike, were all greatly afflicted by this news and began to mourn in the manner described before. Since so many of them came out to the grove of sal trees where the Buddha lay, Ananda had to present them in large family groups instead of one by one. Some editions add that many became lay disciples and, not surprisingly, that the Buddha taught them of the impermanence of all things.

The Buddha's last convert

While the population of Kusinara were swayed with grief, as an anonymous crowd, there was one among them who reflected very carefully about these goings-on. He was named Subhadda, or in Sanskrit Subhadra, and was known as a wandering ascetic of, some say, 120 years. He was much respected by the Mallas and had heard the teachings of many others without committing himself to any of them. Now he heard that the Buddha was about to pass away that very night into his *parinibbana*, or final attainment of nirvana, and recollected an old tradition that the appearance of a Buddha in the world is very rare. With this in mind he decided to put his queries about the doctrine of various teachers to the Buddha in person. When he got to the grove of sal trees however Ananda would not let him approach on the grounds that the Buddha was too weak for debates. Even though he asked three times, which usually brings the desired result, Ananda was firm. Fortunately the Buddha overheard and said that Subhadda might step forward, since his enquiries were undoubtedly most important.

Subhadda certainly raised quite a problem for he pointed out that there were several leading religious personages well known at that time, each with their disciples and their doctrine. Six of these are named and some are known to have existed historically. They are referred to elsewhere in Buddhist writings too. Perhaps the most famous of the six was Nigantha Nataputta, who is otherwise known as Mahavira, the founder of the Jain religion. All of them had teachings broadly analogous to that of the Buddha, including some view of the nature of karma and rebirth and the attainment of freedom. They were not expounded in detail on this occasion however, even though Subhadda wanted to know whether they were right or wrong. They all claimed to have understood, he said, but had they? The Buddha declined to enter into controversy over the various views held by all those teachers. He proposed a single criterion. Whatever doctrine and discipline contained within it the 'noble eightfold path' could lead to the four states of saintliness, namely, stream-winner, once-returner, never returner, and arahant. Whatever system did not contain the eightfold path would lead to none of these. The systems of all the other leaders named simply did not produce saints. Subhadda seems to have been convinced by this argument, for he requested ordination by 'the three refuges'. Normally there was a four month probation period for entrants who had previously followed some other doctrine, and Subhadda declared himself willing to accept this condition. As a reward for his good attitude, the condition was thereupon at once withdrawn. In the Pali edition Ananda receives the new monk for ordination, but in some others it is the Buddha himself who ordains him personally with the phrase

'Come, monk!' We are told that Subhadda thereafter made rapid progress and quickly attained the perfected state of an arahant.

The Buddha's reply to Subhadda's question about the different religious systems is of some interest as indicating the Buddhist attitude towards 'other' religions. This is a tricky subject in itself, and in many ways Buddhism tolerates the coexistence of other religions in a most commendable manner. At the same time the story of Subhadda's conversion displays a certain simplistic self-assertion which often characterises the presentation of Buddhism, rather on the lines that 'They are right – provided they agree with me.' In a sense this is the natural self-expression of a great religious leader who has given up trying to follow a variety of paths and simply relies on the discovery of his own experience. This view is confirmed by a couple of verses attributed to the Buddha, in which he declares that he renounced the world when he was twenty-nine and had wandered for fifty-one years thereafter. In that time he had established the true principles of spiritual attainment, apart from which there was simply no possibility of success. It is these figures of twenty-nine and fifty-one which add up to the figure of eighty years mentioned earlier, and reckoned to be the length of the Buddha's life. By this time the reader will have realised that details such as the exact time and place of his journeys, and figures like these about his age, are of rather low historical probability. On the other hand there is a tremendous weight of tradition about the Buddha's last days, which must have some historical meaning in terms of his character and impact.

11

The Buddha Enters Nirvana

Last instructions

Earlier in the story it is told how the Buddha had rejected the idea of giving last instructions to the monastic order, on the grounds that his teaching had always been completely open and was self-sufficient as already made known. Nevertheless in the later portions of the narrative there are certain instructions and last words which perhaps do not contravene the spirit of what had been said before. Some of these appear in rather scattered contexts, and the editions disagree. So here we follow the trend of the Sanskrit edition which tends to draw them together towards the end.

One of the things which Ananda the disciple wanted to know was what should be done with the Buddha's remains when he had died. At first the Buddha would not say what should be done, on the grounds that the monks ought not to be distracted from their own serious endeavours by such a matter. There were plenty of wise laymen among the aristocracy and the Brahman caste, who had joined his following, and who would know what to do. When Ananda persisted he was told that the remains of a Tathagata, that is, of a Buddha, should be treated like those of a great benevolent monarch, a 'wheel-turning king'. More details of this will be mentioned later. The main point is that the Buddha's sanction was given to a cult of devotion to his person, centred on his relics. Did he do so, historically? One cannot help but feel that there is an element of later rationalisation here. On the other hand if he ever did discuss such matters during his life-time, it would seem to fit what little we have of a historical picture if he told monks not to bother with such things, but allowed laymen to give expression to their faith in his teaching in the ordinary ways of the time. It is noteworthy that the importance of his remains was put in context by reference to others whose remains should also be honoured. These included those mysterious figures who attained enlightenment on an independent basis (known as *pacceka-buddhas*), and also 'hearers', that is, those who heard and followed the Buddha's way, as well as the great kings mentioned earlier.

Ananda was also still concerned about the effect of the Buddha's absence on his followers, and it is through his questions and the answers given that we can perceive something of what happened to the Buddhist religion at the very end of the Buddha's life. Ananda asked about the monks who used to retreat to their various shelters during the rainy season and then come to the Buddha for audiences at other times. Ananda thought that he and the other monks would no longer be in a position to receive them. After all, if the Buddha were no longer present, how would the various monks know where to go? It was the Buddha himself who provided a localised reference point for the whole monastic movement. It may be that the answer to this question was a later rationalisation of what people ended up by doing in practice, giving it the Buddha's own authority. He called upon them to visit four places which they could associate with him. These were the place of his birth, the place where he attained enlightenment, the place where he had first proclaimed his Dhamma, and the place where he would pass away. These places would serve as a substitute for the Buddha's own person, in the sense that they could be visited with respect. Here there could come monks and nuns, laymen and laywomen. Those who came with a believing heart on one of these pilgrimages, and happened to die on the way, would surely be reborn in a happier, heavenly state. It is noteworthy that this answer was not specifically for the ordained, but also for lay disciples. It illustrates the establishment of a whole new mode of religious practice which would maintain something of the impact of the Buddha's personal presence, if only by recollection.

As to the order itself, the Buddha anticipated that some might think themselves to be without a teacher. It is sometimes put about that he said he would be replaced by the body of his teaching, that is by the Dhamma; but in fact the text refers to Dhamma *and*

Vinaya, that is, teaching *and* discipline. Indeed the Sanskrit edition stresses the role of the fortnightly confession ritual, the *patimokkha* (Sanskrit: *pratimoksha*), as the refuge which would replace the Buddha himself. What is clear is that the Buddha appointed no single successor or representative. The Buddhist following was therefore conceived of along republican lines, so to speak, rather than monarchical ones. There was not even a fixed group of oligarchical leaders. All Buddhist orders in various places constituted themselves in a kind of independent equality with each other. The touchstone, as in the case of the 'four great authorities' referred to before, was inward consistency with the Dhamma and the Vinaya.

The only concession to the hierarchical way of thinking, which seems to emerge again and again in human society, lay in a last-minute rubric on forms of address – if indeed we are to believe the texts. This instruction was that the monks should no longer indiscriminately call each other 'friend'. Senior monks might call junior monks by name, or they might call them 'friend', and they had a responsibility to train them in the Buddhist life. Younger monks on the other hand had to call their seniors 'Sir' or 'Venerable'.

A much more severe instruction was left in connection with women, though it should be pointed out that this famous utterance is only found in some editions. There is an old tradition that the Buddha agreed to the ordination of women with great reluctance, though the fact remains that a female order of nuns really does seem to have been founded during his lifetime. The reader may recall that when the Buddha was visited at Vesali by the courtesan named Ambapali he warned his attendant monks to concentrate carefully because women were approaching. The short passage of instruction about women shows us Ananda asking how the monks should behave towards women. 'As if you do not see them,' was the answer. Ananda pressed the point. 'What if we do see them?' to which the answer was, 'No talking!' And if women themselves address the monks? Then 'Keep wide awake!' This may seem to show the Buddha's attitude towards women to be extremely negative. One should perhaps distinguish however between his acceptance of women as disciples, and the belief that attachment to women on the part of men was a major obstacle in men's attainment of nirvana. The latter seems to be an entirely consistent feature of the Buddha's fundamental understanding of the world.

Among the last instructions was the rather sad case of a monk named Channa, who had behaved badly in some unspecified way. The Buddha said that he should be ignored, indeed 'sent to Coventry', to use the English colloquialism. Again this may seem a harsh judgement such as one would not expect from the Buddha. However it was presumably a kind of self-exclusion, arising out of the simple incompatibility between joining the order and not observing its corporate discipline. Other traditions say that this monk eventually changed his attitude and was accepted again by all. The Sanskrit and some other editions put this particular anecdote at an earlier point in the narrative as a whole, and it may be considered incidental, rather than a vital part of the Buddha's last words. As to discipline in general it is recalled that the Buddha gave permission to the monks to abolish all the 'lesser' and 'minor' precepts. However, it seems that, whatever was referred to as 'lesser' and 'minor', the monks did not avail themselves of this permission; although variations in the code of discipline appeared later and were eventually the cause of some dissension.

The Buddha then asked the whole company assembled whether there were no questions or doubts in their minds. Now was the time to express them. They should not reproach themselves later with the thought that they had missed the opportunity to ask their teacher while he was alive. He was met with a silence. So he asked again, and even a third time, suggesting that if they felt shy of hurting his feelings as their teacher they might put any doubts first to each other. The monks still remained silent. Ananda then said how wonderful it was that there was not one monk in the whole company who had any misgivings about the Buddha's teaching. Through his speech the tradition records its satisfaction that when the Buddha died there was a completely coherent order of monks left behind. As to the Buddha himself, it is recalled that he assured them all that they would certainly attain enlightenment in due course. Again one cannot help but remark the characteristics of literary construction, such as the three-fold enquiry, and the fact that the monks numbered the remarkably round figure of 500. On the other hand it seems incontrovertibly true that the Buddha died in old age on the occasion of some kind of sickness. There must therefore have been some closing scenes in his life such as those described in the narratives.

The Buddha's nirvana

The very last act of the Buddha's life is described with some variations. In some editions the Buddha revealed the upper part of his body in a gesture. Waldschmidt believed that the historical kernel of this was a straightforward demonstration of how sickness and weakness had made even a Buddha's body impermanent. Later versions transpose any such original meaning into something very near its opposite, namely an extremely rare opportunity to see the perfect and resplendent body of a Buddha. Every edition agrees that he declared: 'All compound things are subject to decay.' Some add: 'Strive diligently!' These were the Buddha's final words as he passed away, never to be reborn into suffering again.

He died in a state of meditation described in detail in all the texts. Firstly, he set himself in turn in the four *jhanas* (described earlier). From there he went into five further states of being known as the 'formless *jhanas*' – consciousness only of the infinity of space, consciousness only of the infinity of thought, consciousness of no particular object at all, suspension between consciousness and no-consciousness, and finally a state in which all sensation and consciousness have ceased. Ananda then thought that the Buddha had died, as perhaps the reader may also be suspecting. 'Not so,' said the monk Anuruddha, 'He is simply in a state in which all sensation and consciousness have ceased.' Thereupon the Buddha reversed his meditational exercise right down through all the five 'formless *jhanas*' and through the first four *jhanas*. Then he mounted again, from the first to the second, then to the third, and then again to the fourth *jhana*: a state in which both pain and pleasure are absent, a state of pure awareness and pure equanimity. In this state he breathed his last. In Buddhist terms, he attained nirvana without any remainder.

The moment of the Buddha's death was freely mythologised, with earthquake and thunder. The great gods Brahma and Sakka (Sakra in Sanskrit – another name of Indra) pronounced verses on the transiency of life and the Sanskrit narrative also tells of the sal trees shedding their blossoms. In the real world, it seems quite likely that either Anuruddha or Ananda, or both, made a solemn pronouncement that the Buddha had died. The texts are varied and historical precision is unattainable. Did Anuruddha, the wise and steady monk, announce that the Buddha breathed no more in and no more out, that he had been unshaken by pains, and that he had attained release in final nirvana as when a flame is no longer fuelled? And were they really Ananda's words which spoke of a feeling of terrible dread, when the master with all his supernormal powers was finally alive no longer? We do not really know. Yet the mixture of emotions among the assembled monks is strongly evidenced. On the one hand the Buddha had successfully completed his path, which was therefore cause for respectful observation rather than regret or sorrow. On the other hand the human impact of the man over the years certainly left a sense of loss among the more dependent disciples. The advanced monks, the arahants, reflected on the Buddha's own teaching of the impermanence of all compounded things. For them the Buddha was a model of the path on which they too were already far progressed. Other monks mourned openly, stretching out their arms and falling on the ground as they wept. For them the Buddha was more than a theoretical model. He was also an emotional support, giving confidence that their abandonment of worldly life would eventually lead to a great sense of peace. For these the Buddha had died much too soon. Anuruddha tried to calm them, stressing the Buddha's own teaching of impermanence, and recalling the discussion of previous days about spirits who mourn and spirits who do not mourn.

So the monks talked with each other until morning came. Then Anuruddha requested Ananda to go into the town of Kusinara and tell the people that the Buddha had died. Ananda arranged his robe, took up his bowl, and went off with one other monk into the town.

Relics

The people of Kusinara were much affected by the news, and they certainly belonged among those who mourn. They came in a great crowd to the grove of sal trees where the Buddha's body lay. They brought garlands of flowers, played music and sang, set up decorated canopies between the trees and perfumed the air with delicate scents. This lasted all day until it was much too late to perform a cremation. The same happened the next day, and the next, until six whole days had passed.

On the seventh day they set about the cremation. At first they thought they would take the body to a spot south of the city, but eventually it was carried to a holy spot named Makutabandhana, east of the city. All these events are described in a tone of considerable excitement and with supernatural agencies playing their part.

The model for the funeral preparations was that of a 'wheel-turning monarch'. The Mallas' leaders asked how it should be done, and Ananda repeated the instructions given previously to him by the Buddha. First the body was wrapped in cloth and then in combed raw cotton, then in cloth again, then raw cotton again, and so on for 500 layers of each. It was placed in an iron vessel containing oil, which was covered over with another similar vessel as a lid. This was placed on a funeral pyre of sweet smelling woods. The remains would be placed at the base of a memorial mound or stupa to be raised at the nearest cross-roads to the site of cremation.

The ceremony was delayed until another leading monk, Maha Kassapa, had arrived from Pava, with a great company of monks. Some of these were greatly distressed by the news of the Buddha's death, while others bore it with the equanimity appropriate to his own teaching of transience. One elderly monk refused to mourn at all for another reason. He argued that they were well rid of the man who made so many rules for them. Now they could do what they liked. The unexpectedness of this point of view makes it entirely likely that it really was maintained by one monk, or a few monks. The Pali edition, alone, names him Subhadda, but presumably this does not imply identity with the Subhadda whose story was told before. Other editions give other names, or no name.

When the newly arrived monks had paid their last respects, by bowing down with folded hands, walking round the pyre three times and bowing at the Buddha's feet, the pyre was set alight. All was burned away except for the bones, and the fire was ceremoniously extinguished. The various editions all introduce miraculous elements, such as that the fire lit itself, that the inner-most and outermost garments were not burned, and that the fire was quenched by streams of water from the heavens. Historically however it is clear that the funeral followed the main pattern of Indian cremation ritual. Another seven days the bones were kept in state by the Mallas. Normally the bones would be washed and placed into an urn. The story stresses that no ash or soot re-mained attached to them.

While the Mallas carried the ceremonies through, the news of the Buddha's death had travelled. Ajatasattu the king of Magadha sent a messenger to claim the relics on the grounds that he too was a member of the warrior caste. Not surprisingly there were others who made the same claim, such as the Licchavis of Vesali and the Malla people of Pava, where the Buddha had recently been. The texts also include the Sakyas of Kapilavatthu, who argued that the Buddha had belonged to their people. And of course the Mallas of Kusinara were not anxious to give up the precious remains, for after all the Buddha had passed away in their territory. It was left to a diplomatic Brahman named Dona to divide the relics into eight equal parts for the contending parties, who numbered eight in all. The Moriyas of Pipphalivana sent a messenger who arrived too late, and so they had to be content with embers from the funeral fire. The eight portions of relics were taken off to the cities of the peoples round about and memorial mounds were built over them. The Brahman himself received the urn in which the relics had first been placed, and he went off to build a mound over that, in his own village.

These mounds were an essential part of the beginning of the Buddhist religion, for it was said that anyone who went to place flowers, perfume or decorative paint before them, or simply to bow in reverence or to experience peace of heart, would surely reap benefit from so doing. This was one of the main ways in which the devotional attitude towards the Buddha was fostered among monks and lay people alike.

PART FOUR

MYTH

12

The Buddha's Life-Pattern

Causes of an earthquake

As the story of the Buddha's life took shape it grew up on certain patterns which can still be discerned in embryo form. One of the most important of these was the continued working over of the two main clusters of text dealing with the Buddha's enlightenment and nirvana. It is quite striking that for centuries nobody took what might seem the obvious step of running these two stories together into one life story. There are some indications that these two events were considered to be the most important of all. For one thing they are described as the two events when a Buddha's body glows brightly, as when the young man Pukkusa gave the Buddha robes of shimmering gold cloth which seemed to lose their lustre by comparison. Similarly Chunda the metal-smith was to be told not to feel remorseful about giving the Buddha food which made him ill, for there are two meals which are particularly meritorious: that which a Buddha takes just after his enlightenment, and that which he takes just before his final nirvana.

The two reference points, enlightenment and nirvana, came to be taken up into fuller patterns. The four goals of pilgrimage for example are defined as:

(1) the place where the Buddha was born;
(2) the place where he attained enlightenment;
(3) the place where he first expounded the Dhamma, and
(4) the place where he passed away.

These four begin to offer the skeleton of a life-story.

When we come on to the eight causes of an earthquake more elements are brought in. The first two explain earthquakes which are not connected with the Buddha. The earth floats on a great expanse of water which in turn is borne aloft on a mighty wind, it is said, below which is empty space. When the wind blows, the water moves and the earth shakes. The second possible cause is that a very spiritual hermit might concentrate in his mind on a tiny speck of earth and a great stretch of water, both at once; this can make the earth tremble. All the other six causes of earthquakes are events in the life of a Buddha as follows:

1. A Buddha-to-be leaves the heavens to enter his mother's womb;
2. The Buddha-to-be is born;
3. He attains enlightenment (becomes a Buddha);
4. The Buddha proclaims Dhamma for the first time;
5. The Buddha rejects a possible prolongation of his life;
6. The Buddha passes away without residue.

This extended conception of a Buddha's life is not biographical, it will be noted, but mythological. In particular the life-pattern is extended back before the Buddha's birth. But all the events have a religious meaning which is more important than the mere historical or biographical point to which they are related. And each is attended by an earthquake.

Other Buddhas

The idea that the Buddha's life followed a certain pattern was strongly reinforced by the belief that it was parallel in principle to that of various previous Buddhas. The canonical writings contain stories of these Buddhas, giving their names, the names of their birthplace, parents, caste and clan, chief disciples and personal attendant, and other details such as the usual length of life lived at the time. In the case of 'our' historical Buddha, the birth-place is given as Kapilavatthu, his father is named King Suddhodana, his mother is named Maya and the expected life-span was one hundred years (which he consciously shortened to eighty). He was a member of the Kshatriya or warrior caste and belonged to the Gotama clan. The chief disciples were Sariputta and Moggallana, and the attendant disciple was Ananda. Quite apart from these details a stereotyped phrase refers, for each Buddha, to leaving the world, becoming a hermit, practising austerities, attaining enlightenment and preaching the Dhamma. When the story is told in detail it begins with the miraculous descent from the heavens, includes infancy and youth stories and then leads into the enlightenment and first teaching. The same story applies, with different names and other details, to every single Buddha. It has become, therefore, a normative myth.

The implication of this is that when we read the story of prodigious feats by the newly born Buddha-to-be, it is no more nor less true for 'our' historical Buddha, than it is for the ancient Buddha named Vipassi, who lived ninety-one aeons ago. In those days the expected life-span was not a mere 100 years but 80,000 years, Vipassi's father was named King Bandhuma and his mother was named Bandhumati, and so on. Since the extended life story of the 'historical' Buddha, as opposed to all other Buddhas past and future, still follows this same pattern wherever it is found, it can only be treated as a mythologised account devised in retrospect. It does not add any new history.

A common thread

The most important anecdotes of this expanded story, which is found in several different writings, will be given below. First however one more observation is necessary. In spite of the astonishing elaborations which took place, there remained for centuries a tendency to tell the tale from birth (or just before) up to the enlightenment and first teaching. In other words it led up to the founding of Buddhism as a religion. The nativity and youth stories represent a massive preamble to enlightenment narratives such as those already considered. That is why the *Mahavastu*, which is an immense elaboration of the whole theme, is known to us as part of the books of *discipline* of one of the ancient sects. Its position is basically analogous to that of the *Mahavagga* in the Theravada books of discipline. Other extended writings such as the *Nidana-katha* (introduction to the Pali books of *jatakas*), the *Lalitavistara* (a late Sanskrit work), and the *Buddhacarita* (a well-known poetic version in Sanskrit), are similar in that they leave us with the Buddha alive and well, at the height of his activity.

This is not just accidental, for the Buddhists spoke of three kinds of 'occasion' which gave rise to Buddhist teaching or discipline. There was the 'proximate occasion' of the Buddha's first decision to teach and the first ordinations. There was the general cause of all his work, the 'non-distant occasion', namely the whole story of the Buddha's life from his descent into the world up to his enlightenment. And, thirdly, there was the 'distant occasion' which threw the story back into distant ages when the Buddha-to-be was still an individual in training, while other Buddhas proclaimed the Dhamma. Thus the main story of the Buddha's life from his birth to the founding point of the Buddhist religion consisted of the 'non-distant occasion' and the 'proximate occasion', and this conception accounts for its stability as a literary form.

Meanwhile the nirvana story was circulating in its own right, as a separate and very well-known work. It was not until the third or fourth century AD that a complete life of the Buddha was offered from beginning to end. On the other hand the idea of the four places of pilgrimage includes the Buddha's birth, his spiritual achievement, first teaching and death. Similarly, a brief summary in the *Buddhavamsa*, which tells of twenty-four previous Buddhas, also refers to the Buddha's birthplace and family, achievements *and* final nirvana. Interestingly enough the commentary (*Maduratthavilasini*) gives a more detailed story which only seems to go as far as the opening of the Buddha's public activity, that is, it is still based on the idea of the 'non-distant occasion' and the 'proximate occasion'. Nevertheless the existence of some embryo patterns running from the Buddha's birth right through to his death shows that it is not entirely out of tune with the early Buddhist mentality to think of the Buddha's life as a whole, whether historically as at the beginning of this book, or more mythologically, as now towards the end.

The main sources for the mythologised life-story of the Buddha diverge and overlap in many complicated ways. A comparative analysis would be quite unreadable, and therefore the main anecdotes are given below in summary form. The reader must be prepared for variations, if the story is met with again in other sources; but this method is quite adequate to give a fair impression of the main outline current all over Asia.

13

Birth of a Prince

Decision to be born a Buddha

The idea that the story of the Buddha began with his birth is not quite appropriate to the mythologising Buddhist mind. The 'non-distant occasion' begins with the Buddha-to-be, or bodhisatta (Sanskrit: bodhisattva), pleasantly dwelling in the heavens, having served an extremely long apprenticeship under former Buddhas in his previous existences. The angels and gods who dwell in these heavens know when it is time for a Buddha to appear, and also know which bodhisatta is about to be reborn to be the Buddha. They therefore beseech him to do so, and he himself, pretending to take no notice, considers the details of his imminent birth.

Five aspects of his birth are attended to. The first is the time. Since people do not listen to the teaching of impermanence, suffering and non-self when they live a long time, and since they are too sinful when life is short, it is necessary to be born when people live for a hundred years or more. As to the place, Buddhas are always born in India (known as Jambudvipa), of which the most appropriate part was the 'Middle Country'. This was regarded as the centre of the known world. Within it the town of Kapilavatthu seemed appropriate. Of the available classes of people the warrior (Kshatriya) caste seemed to be of best repute, and the chief or king of these at Kapilavatthu, named Suddhodana, was selected as his father. His mother was to be very virtuous indeed, and the chosen lady was named Maya. Her life was foreseen to have but ten months and seven days to run.

Since the Buddha-to-be thus consciously selected not only his time and place of birth, but also his parents, it is not surprising that Maya's conception of him is miraculously viewed. At the time of full moon during the midsummer festival she rose early and bathed, lay down on her royal bed and dreamed that she was carried away to the Himalaya mountains. Here she was bathed again by angel queens, to ensure that she was free from all worldly impurity, and laid down on a celestial couch in a golden house on a silent hill. There the Buddha-to-be approached in the form of a white elephant, carrying a white lotus flower with his trunk. He tapped Maya's right side and thereby was instantly incarnated in her womb.

When the queen awoke she told the king, who immediately summoned four Brahmans, treated them to lavish hospitality and asked them to explain the queen's dream. They predicted that the child would be a boy, and that in due course he would either become a 'wheel-turning' monarch, a universal king, or, if he renounced the world for the religious life he would become a Buddha and free mankind from ignorance.

At the moment of the Buddha's conception there was a tremendous earthquake, the story says, and many other unusual events. The deaf heard, the dumb spoke, the lame walked and prisoners were set free. The earth was filled with flowers and sweet scents, and musical instruments played by themselves. The Buddha-to-be was visible in the mother's womb, like a thread in a transparent gem. But the womb in which a future Buddha has dwelled (usually represented upright and fully formed) cannot thereafter be the home of an ordinary mortal. For this reason the mother died seven days after giving birth, and was herself reborn in a celestial realm. For this reason too the Buddha-to-be had selected a woman whose remaining length of life was exactly ten months and seven days, ten months being counted for the time of pregnancy. (Ten lunar months are 280 days, which, if counted from the day after the period preceding conception, comes to about the same as nine months of thirty days counted from between periods). It is traditional to count pregnancy as ten months in Asia, and the number has no special mythological significance.

The birth

The queen wished to give birth at her home town of Devadaha which was some way off from Kapilavatthu. The king agreed, had the road made ready and sent off the queen in a golden palanquin with a great retinue. On the way they passed a beautiful woodland of sal trees called Lumbini. Here the queen wished to rest. The wood was filled with flowers and fruits, birds and bees. As she came to the largest tree, she stretched out her hand to take hold of one of the branches which suddenly bent itself towards her. She felt the labour pains coming on, the people drew a curtain round her and retired, and there, standing up and holding the branch in her hand, she gave birth.

The baby was born without any of the usual blood or impurities, coming out miraculously from Maya's right side, standing up on his feet, shining like a jewel. Angels placed him on a roll of fine cloth, men and angels offered him sweetly scented garlands, and he surveyed the universe in all directions. Seeing no rivals, he took seven strides and called out with a voice like a lion 'I am the chief of the world. I am supreme in the world. This is my last existence. Henceforth, there is no more rebirth for me.' This is known as the 'Song of victory'.

On the same day there came into existence several other persons who feature in the Buddha's story. These included the princess Yasodhara whom he later married (other names also current), Channa his attendant, a minister named Kaludayi, his horse named Kanthaka, and the great pipal tree (a large banyan-like fig tree) under which he would one day sit and achieve enlightenment. It is as if all the actors in the play were assembled together on the appropriate day.

The king was advised at that time by a religious hermit, so advanced that he was able to spend the heat of the day in one of the heavens normally inhabited only by angels. His name was Kala Devala, (or otherwise Asita). As he sat and rested he saw the angels rejoicing, asked them the reason, and hurried back to the king's palace to see the king's new son. The boy was expected to pay homage to the holy man with his matted hair, but instead the latter paid homage. Otherwise, it is said, the ascetic's head would have split in two. The holy man could see into past and future and realised that the boy was to become a Buddha. He also knew within himself that he was due to be reborn in the 'formless world' before that would happen. Since he would therefore never see the Buddha as a Buddha, he wept.

Naturally the people were perturbed. Kala Devala explained

what the future held, and persuaded at least a relative of his, a nephew named Nalaka, to take up the homeless life, so that he could one day become the Buddha's disciple. Nalaka did so, put on yellow clothes, shaved his head and set off carrying a bowl. He lived for many years in the Himalayas and eventually returned to be the Buddha's disciple. After that he went back again to the Himalayas, lived another seven months and then passed away into final nirvana without remainder.

When the seer is named Asita, the story also brings in the special marks which he observes the baby to possess, and which indicate his destiny. Lists of these thirty-two special marks vary somewhat from text to text, but they influenced Buddhist sculpture through the ages from India to Japan. Most of the characteristics add up to a particularly evenly balanced and well formed body, with 'antelope limbs', even shoulders, perfect teeth, eyes and voice and so on. The body hairs are black, rise one from each pore and curl to the right. More especially one may note the soles of his feet which are marked with wheels of a thousand spokes. (These appear in sculptures of the Buddha in the nirvana position). Another prominent characteristic is the protuberance at the top of the head, his head being shaped 'like a turban', which may have originated as a knot of tied-up hair.

On the fifth day after the Buddha-to-be was born a name-giving ceremony was held. The name selected by King Suddhodana was Siddhattha. The main point of the story however lies in the predictions of Brahmans called to the palace for this occasion. No less than 108 of these priestly persons were invited to attend, all well versed in the *Vedas*, the ancient holy books of India. The king's house was decked out in flowers and well scented with perfumes, pleasant food was served, and eight of the Brahmans were asked to declare the boy's future. Seven of them held up two fingers to indicate two alternative destinies. Either he would become a 'wheel-turning' monarch, or, if he renounced the world, he would become a Buddha. The eighth Brahman, however, the youngest, and also the holiest, held up one finger only, declaring that he would certainly become a Buddha. This Brahman was called Kondanna. The other seven persuaded Kondanna to take up a hermit's life there and then, and before long they themselves died and were reborn in accordance with their karma. Kondanna did become a hermit, came before long to a pleasant place named Uruvela, took up with four companions, and thus was the leader of the group of five to whom the Buddha eventually first gave his teaching.

The king himself was more interested in the alternative destiny prophesied for his son by the other seven. What might be the cause, he enquired, of his son's renouncing the world? For whatever it was, he would strive to ensure its absence. The Brahmans declared that the cause of his renouncing the world would be the four signs: a man worn with age, a sick man, a dead body, and a homeless ascetic. These would be the stimulus which would make the young man leave home. The king resolved that his son should never see these things and so might win instead the extensive temporal power of a universal monarch. It was not that he was against the religious life, but considered from a practical point of view there was the question of the succession. Guards were set all round over a diameter of two miles so that no disturbing persons might approach his son.

The conflict of intentions set up in the story has a distinct dramatic force, even though the decision to be born as a Buddha had been taken already in the mythological beginning of the story. There is a tension between glory with power and wealth on one hand, and the search to identify underlying reality on the other. Could the king prevent his son from coming into contact with the true character of human experience?

Childhood

The most common childhood story about the Buddha-to-be is the incident at a ploughing festival organised by the king, in which a thousand ploughs were set to till the ground. The king himself drove a ceremonial ox-team with harness and plough decorated in red gold. In the meantime the boy was set on a couch beneath a tree, thick with leaves and giving dense shade. Above him was a canopy, and round about a curtain. The king went off to plough, his ministers also playing their parts with silver-decorated ploughs. Even the attendant nurses stole out to see the ceremony or competition and the young child was left to himself. Noticing this he got up from the lying position, seated himself cross-legged, controlled his breathing and settled in the first *jhana* (a trance-like meditational state, referred to earlier). As the time passed, the attendants were preparing food outside, the sun moved round and the shadows lengthened. Only the shadow of the tree under which the child sat was unmoved, cast in a circular form all round beneath the tree. When the nurses looked inside the tent again they saw the posture adopted by the Buddha-to-be, noticed also the miracle of the tree's shadow which still shaded him, and reported it all to the king. The king paid homage to his son, as he had also done before when the holy man Asita had done so.

Some versions of this story bring in five holy men, who were flying through the air from the Himalayas (by means of the supernormal powers ascribed to holy men in ancient India), but who could not pass this spot and thus were forced to come down to pay reverence. Sometimes it is not just the first *jhana* which the child is said to have attained, but all four *jhanas*.

Another story of the Buddha's early childhood is that he was to be taken to the temple to be presented to the gods. When he heard of this proposal he pointed out that he had already received the title of *devatideva,* 'god beyond gods', from the gods themselves, and therefore there was little purpose in it. However, he conformed to the convention, and when he set foot in the temple the images of all the gods there arrayed fell down and broke. At this there was derisive laughter from all sides.

Next, ornaments were made for him at the instigation of the king's family priest named Udayana. No less than 500 different ornaments of all kinds were prepared, golden and bejewelled, but when they were placed upon the young prince they seemed to lose all their lustre. They were simply eclipsed by the radiance of his own person.

Similarly when it was decided that he should learn to write, he was taken to a writing master and set down before him, pen in hand. Needless to say, he had a sandalwood tablet, the very best ink, and a golden pen. The interview began when the Buddha-to-be asked the writing teacher which alphabet he was to be taught. He then reeled off a list of sixty-four different writing systems, Indian, Chinese and entirely mythological kinds used by supernatural beings. The very fact that he had prior knowledge of what all these were was enough to make his teacher recognise him as a being beyond the gods. When all the other boys began to learn the Sanskrit alphabet, a, ā, i, ī, u, ū, etc., the Buddha-to-be used each letter to expound a religious truth as for example 'a is for *anicca* (impermanence). The tradition that single letters or syllables have a hidden power or meaning is an ancient tradition in India, and once taken over in this way by Buddhism it was passed on to other Buddhist countries far away, such as Japan.

Early manhood

An element common to the traditions is that the king had three palaces built for his son, now nearly grown up. One was for the cold season, one was for the hot season, and one was for the rainy season; and one was nine storeys high, one was seven storeys high and one was five storeys high. Here the prince lived surrounded by so many dancing girls that one scarcely dares to repeat the number (40,000). Musical instruments played themselves.

Sometimes the story is that he lived here with his wife until his countrymen began to murmur that he lived for pleasure only and had no ability in the skills required of manhood. Sometimes the story is that only through feats of physical prowess could he win the hand of his wife Yasodhara, (or else Bhaddakacca, or Gopa). One of the longer stories tells of the prince's own requirements for his future wife, a massive reception of young ladies from the Sakya families and his personal selection of Gopa, with the gift of a dazzling ring. In this longer story, (the *Lalitavistara*), the prince then proved himself not only in archery by stringing a bow so strong that nobody else could string it, but also by wrestling and by feats of mathematical calculation.

Another tension is introduced when his envious cousin Devadatta slew a great white elephant intended for the prince's use, and left it for dead at the city gate. Another prince drew the dead beast aside from the gate, but the Buddha-to-be, seeing it lying there, picked it up with his big toe and twirled it through the air, high across the city, so that it landed two miles away on the other side. The crater which it made became known as Elephant's Hollow. This clash with Devadatta anticipates a rivalry important at a later stage in the developed legend.

In the meantime the prince was safely esconced in his palaces with every need fulfilled. King Suddhodana ensured by his commands that nothing untoward should ever meet his son's eyes, no old age, no sickness, no death. Nothing should awaken in his mind the idea of becoming a mendicant monk.

14

Renunciation

The four signs

Since the king had placed his guards at two mile intervals and the young prince suspected nothing of the real nature of the world, even though he was a superman, it was necessary for the gods to take a hand. It really seemed as though the prince would proceed along his royal road until he finally became a universal monarch ruling the whole known world. One day however he wished to drive in his pleasure gardens. The charioteer set up his chariot in the most beautiful trappings, four state horses were harnessed, each as white as a white lotus, and off they drove to the park. This was still within the secluded area allowed by the king, but the devas, the angel-like gods of the Indian heavens, decided to take this opportunity to break through the king's guard.

This they did by making one of their number appear in the form of a very old man by the wayside. His body was bent and wasted, his teeth and hair quite decayed, and he could only hold himself up with a stick. Only the prince and the charioteer could see him, so the former asked the latter who he was and why he was in that condition. The charioteer replied that the man was an aged man with not much longer to live. The prince then asked naïvely whether he too would one day be so aged and worn, and when he heard that this came to all men he demanded that they turn back at once to the palace. The king heard of this incident and ordered all manner of music and drama to be laid on, in the hope that these interests would distract the prince from his reflections. The guards were increased and placed at closer intervals.

Some time passed and the prince again went driving in the pleasure gardens. This time the devas showed one of themselves as a very sick man, helpless by himself and being attended to by others. Once again the prince asked why this should be, and was told that disease can strike at all living people. Again he returned home at once, deeply disturbed, and again the king increased the guard and redoubled the amusement programme.

Again time passed (though sometimes these encounters are all said to have taken place on the same day), until the prince went driving once more. This time the gods acted a crowd of people getting ready a funeral pyre. When this was explained he wished to see the corpse of the dead man, and the charioteer obliged by driving close by. 'What does dying mean?' he asked, and was told that it means that one is no more seen by parents and relations, and that one never again sees them. Even the prince himself was certain to die, he heard, just like all other people. Back he went to the palace and brooded over these matters. What was the point of being born, he wondered, if old age and disease and death are brought upon us?

Finally the prince drove out for a fourth time, and this time though seeing nothing untoward they did pass by a man with shaven head and a yellow robe. Till then the charioteer himself had never seen such a man, but the devas inspired him to explain that the man was a wandering monk. Or else the monk explained himself that he had 'gone forth', which meant that he had abandoned household life and practised an existence of complete harmlessness and kindness to all living beings. The prince resolved there and then that he would do the same. He sent his charioteer home and rested in the pleasure garden to think things over. In the meantime the god Sakka felt the seat upon which he sat in the heavens become warm, which meant that he had a task to do. Realising that the prince was about to renounce the world he sent another deva named Vissakamma to arrange his hair in a turban. Although Vissakamma appeared in the form of the royal barber the prince could sense the touch of the gods.

Resolve

Rested, bathed and coiffured, the prince remounted his chariot, when word came that his wife had given birth to a son. There followed one of the most painful moments in the Buddha's life story, for he reacted by saying, 'A fetter has been born.' This was reported to the king who then announced, trying no doubt to make the best of this disappointing response, that the name of his grandson should therefore be Rahula (meaning 'fetter'). Usually people rejoice over the birth of their children, and in oriental countries generally there is special importance attached to the birth of boys, particularly in royal families. By naming his son Rahula the prince effectively declared his whole royal and family life to be a 'hindrance'. It was therefore a dramatic form of personal renunciation, indeed of rejection.

As he travelled back through the city a beautiful young aristocratic woman named Kisa Gotami caught sight of him and called out a flattering song. The words declared that happy indeed must be the mother, the father, and the wife of so handsome a prince. But the prince thought to himself that such happiness must be temporary indeed. Only when passion and hatred and pride had ceased could there be a real inward peace. And once again he resolved to renounce the world with its household cares and seek to attain this peace, or nirvana. Since the beautiful girl's song had been the cause of this train of thought he took a precious string of pearls from his neck and had it sent up to her. Naturally enough she failed to understand what had been in his mind and flattered herself with the thought that he had fallen in love with her.

Back in the palace, he was surrounded by beautiful women as he lay on his couch. They danced and sang in various arrangements, enough to enchant anybody, but the prince was no longer interested and simply fell asleep. Seeing this, the women put aside their instruments and theatrical accessories and went to sleep themselves. The prince then awoke a little later, sat up cross-legged and surveyed the scene. Their dress was disordered, some had their mouths open, others were muttering in their sleep. To the prince's mind the palace seemed to be a house full of potential corpses. The women were nothing but a source of mental anguish. Life itself seemed to be like a house on fire with passions, a house from which one should quickly depart. So once again he resolved to leave the world, and this time he got up and went to the door. Calling out to his charioteer, named Channa, he told him that he was resolved that very night to carry through his 'great renunciation'. Channa should saddle him a horse.

The horse he selected was a mighty beast named Kanthaka, who felt the saddle being tightly arranged and knew that it was for his master to ride off and renounce the world. At this he gave a great neigh which would have been heard all over the town had the devas not muffled the sound.

One thing the prince allowed himself, and that was to take one last look at his son Rahula. There he lay with his mother beside him on a bed strewn with jasmine flowers. His mother's hand rested on his head and so the prince dared not pick him up. If he had woken the wife whom he was about to leave she would undoubtedly have raised the alarm and jeopardised his departure. So instead of taking his baby son in his arms he silently promised to return and see him after he had become a Buddha. So reflecting, he left the palace.

Flight

In some texts, especially the Pali legends, the horse is more important than in others. Indeed he is made to play an important and understanding part in the prince's escape. Equally important were the devas, who muffled the horse's neighing and also placed their hands invisibly beneath his hoofs to stifle the sound of his galloping. We are told that the prince rode on the great horse's back while the charioteer, Channa, had to manage somehow by holding on to the horse's tail. When they came to the city gate at midnight each had a plan, for the king had hundreds of armed men at each gate. The prince was getting ready to leap over the wall on his horse with Channa holding to his tail. The horse anticipated the same. Channa for his part (as well he might) had a different though equally stupendous plan, namely to carry his master on his shoulders, seize the horse round its middle and so leap over the wall. Fortunately, none of these desperately bold intentions was needed, for the gate was swung quietly open by a heavenly deva who guarded it, and they rode straight through.

Next came a brief encounter with the evil demon Mara, in his role as tempter. He appeared in the air before the prince and announced that the symbolic wheel of a universal monarch was due to appear in seven days time, and that the prince should therefore not depart but await his political destiny. He would be sovereign over the 'four continents and two thousand adjacent isles'. The prince would not be shaken. He was resolved instead to become a Buddha and thereby delight 'ten thousand worlds'. Mara was foiled and declared his intent to watch out henceforth for any wrong thought or emotion which might stop the Buddha-to-be.

As he left the city another miracle is said to have taken place. He wished to turn round to look upon it for the last time as it lay behind him, but the moment he wished to do so the whole earth (flat, of course) swivelled round 'like a potter's wheel'. Thus it stayed for a few moments while the Buddha-to-be gazed his fill. At the same time the horse pressed forward so that the prince's flight was not delayed by this momentary leave-taking. The reader may be advised not to puzzle over how this was supposed to be physically possible, or even consistent. The point of the story is once again to bring out the hero's simultaneous awareness of what he was renouncing and his unshakeable resolve to continue on his chosen path.

Progressing beyond the city in this exhilarating dash, speeding to freedom from all entanglements, the three were accompanied by celestial hosts of all kinds; the serpent kings, the winged creatures of the heavens and many others. All did homage with perfumes and garlands. Special flowers rained down from the heaven of the god Indra. Music was heard as if from nowhere, or from everywhere. The great white horse struggled through the clouds of blossoms, and the going was so hard that though so strong he could only manage to go for thirty leagues. Finally they came to a river named Anoma, meaning 'illustrious', which seemed a fitting spot for the symbolic acts of renunciation. They crossed to the farther bank and there upon the silver sand the Buddha-to-be gave his farewell instructions to Channa.

Channa was a follower of great loyalty, and earnestly beseeched to be allowed to become a hermit himself as well. But although he made this request for the statutory three times he was refused. His duty was to take back the prince's horse and personal ornaments and to report to the king and queen that he was well, and to this Channa reluctantly agreed.

The intending mendicant then took his sword and cut off his own flowing hair to a length of two inches. It lay close to his head and curled to the right (which is one of the thirty-two marks of a 'great man'). This act of cutting off hair was so important as a symbol of renunciation that the tradition adds that he never needed to cut his hair or shave his beard again. Moreover, the shorn locks and the crown which he had been wearing he tossed up into the sky, with the wish that if he were really to become a Buddha they should stay there. The god Sakka observed this with his deva-sight, caught them up in a jewelled casket, and whisked them away to the heavens where a stupa was raised over them. Another god miraculously provided appropriate robes, an alms-bowl, a razor (which was perhaps never needed), a needle, a girdle and a sieve for straining live insects out of water. So with all the requirements of a wandering mendicant the Buddha-to-be took his leave.

As to the mighty horse Kanthaka, he realised that he would never see his master again, and died of a broken heart.

Channa's sorrowful return to the city and the palace caused great distress, as may be imagined. The *Buddhacarita* pays special attention to the grief of Yasodhara who was driven out of her mind and fell senseless to the ground. The king organised a mission to get his son to return, but all in vain. Gotama, the Buddha-to-be, had renounced the household life.

15

Battle with Mara

Preliminary anecdotes

Once the Buddha-to-be had renounced his worldly life the mythological story follows in principle the same outlines treated earlier. However it is transformed into a tale of more or less serene progress, illustrated with miracles and leading up to the great battle with the demon Mara.

First he journeyed, with miraculous speed, to Rajagaha where he began to beg for food from door to door. His appearance made such an impression of beauty that the populace were stunned by it. Guards went to tell the king, Bimbisara, and suggested it might be a supernatural being in human form. The king ordered that they should observe how he took his food, for this would indicate whether or not he was human. Here comes the human touch – for the food which he had collected suddenly seemed quite inedible. He was nauseated, never having seen such coarse scraps in his life before. But having envied the mendicant's way of life he was now determined to stick to it, and so, repulsive though it was, he finally managed to get the food down. Once the king knew that he was human he went to see him in person. He was so impressed that he offered to abdicate in his favour, but the bodhisatta insisted that he had left everything in order to win enlightenment. All the king could get from him was the promise to come first to the kingdom of Magadha after he had attained his goal.

Gotama's time with other ascetic mendicants is still a part of the mythologised story, though the effects are heightened. When fasting, for example, the devas fed him on a life-giving juice through the pores of his skin. Notwithstanding this assistance he became very thin, lost the golden colour of his skin, lost indeed all the thirty-two marks of a 'great man', and finally fell down as if dead. At this certain of the heavenly devas went off to report his death to his father, King Suddhodana. The king immediately wanted to know whether he had died after attaining Buddhahood or before, and on hearing that he had died before, in the course of his strivings, the king refused to believe it. When his son had abandoned the world the king had recalled the early miraculous incidents of his son's infancy. His confidence was vindicated when Gotama recovered consciousness, which was also reported by devas to the king. When Gotama resumed living on ordinary food the thirty-two marks reappeared.

Near Uruvela, where Gotama had settled for his religious search, there was a special tree of imposing appearance, presumed to be the dwelling of a tree-god. To this tree-god a woman named Sujata had vowed to give a yearly offering if her first-born child proved to be a son. Since it did turn out to be a son she made her offering every year in May at full moon. The offering consisted of rice cooked in milk from the very best of her extensive herds, but this year its preparation was attended by various miracles such as the cows being milked automatically and the fire being lit of itself, or rather by the god Sakka. Sujata was filled with premonitions as a result of these wonders and sent off her slave-girl to keep watch at the sacred tree itself.

In the meantime the Buddha-to-be had dreamed five dreams which led him to think that he would become a Buddha that very day. He was up early, washed and robed, and sat beneath the tree until it would be time to beg for food. Such was the radiance of his appearance, lighting up the whole eastern quarter, that the slave-girl thought it was the tree-god seated there to receive her mistress's offering in person. This she reported to Sujata who was so enchanted at this thought that she declared her slave-girl to be from that time her eldest daughter. The food was placed in a gold vessel and Sujata went herself to the tree. The earthenware begging-bowl provided originally by a deva disappeared from Gotama's grasp, and instead he received the golden bowl with its offering. Sujata then called a blessing on his head, still thinking him to be the tree-god, and departed leaving the precious bowl behind as if it were worth no more than a dead leaf. The Buddha-to-be for his part took the bowl of food down to the nearby river, washed and robed himself again, and then partook of the food dividing it into forty-nine small balls of rice. These forty-nine were to last his body during the forty-nine days (seven times seven) which he spent beneath the tree of enlightenment.

Again Siddhattha the ex-prince tested his destiny. He would place the bowl in the stream, and if he was to become a Buddha that day it should flow up-stream. If not, then let it just flow downstream. As befits the story, it floated upstream; but not only that, it eventually disappeared into a whirlpool and arrived at the under-water palace of the Black Snake King. There it joined company with the special bowls from which three earlier Buddhas had eaten, striking resonantly against them deep beneath the surface. The underlying idea is that the Buddha represents a recurrently valid mythic reality, and this is symbolised by the story-telling technique of various Buddhas doing the same things in the same places.

As the time drew near the Buddha-to-be proceeded, 'like a roused lion' to the tree of enlightenment. Heavenly flowers fell about him and ten thousand worlds were filled with perfume. A grass-cutter, named Sotthiya, gave him some bundles of grass which he took for his seat, and so he approached the tree where he would sit. When one sits beneath a tree one is inescapably limited by a choice of direction. This choice was now given a cosmic setting as Gotama tried each of the four cardinal points. At the southern, western and northern sides the earth seemed to tip down so that the opposite horizon swung up into the air. It seemed to be like a cart-wheel resting on its protruding axle-piece at the centre while someone stands at various points on the rim, tipping up the other side. Only in the eastern quarter was this not so, and therefore Gotama selected here his spot. The sheaves of grass formed themselves magically into an exquisite seat of generous proportions, and there the Buddha-to-be took up his position, his back to the tree, facing due east. It was in this very spot, we are told, that previous Buddhas had long ago won their enlightenment, a spot where the earth was as solid as could be. Gotama sat down cross-legged 'as if welded with a hundred thunderbolts'. Until he attained enlightenment, he vowed, even if his body shrivelled up completely, he would not shift from that spot.

Mara's attacks

Along with the birth and infancy stories the tale of Mara's attacks on the would-be Buddha is one of the most extravagantly elaborated later traditions and has no basis whatever in history. It is cast in entirely mythological terms and does not appear in the earlier accounts, though its development can to some extent be traced back within Buddhist writings. In principle the battle with Mara is a mythological account of a psychological event. One might go on to say that there was originally in the Buddha's personal life some psychological event corresponding to that here mythologised, but unfortunately we have no historical evidence for it.

Mara is the arch-demon of all demons. Seeing that Gotama, or Siddhattha, was about to escape his power entirely, he sounded a great drum and brought out all his hosts for the final battle. Apart from having an army of fierce beings stretching for many miles all round him, Mara himself was mounted on an elephant of monstrous proportions, and he wielded weapons of all kinds with a thousand arms projected especially for the occasion.

In the meantime various well-intentioned and senior gods came to praise Siddhattha's efforts. Sakka had a huge trumpet which collected up the wind by itself and blew out a mighty sound. The Black Snake King stood by and recited fulsome verses. Even the great god Brahma held an official white canopy over the yogi's head. Alas, they could not withstand the concerted attack of Mara's army. All the gods fled away to the mysterious realms which they usually inhabit, leaving Siddhattha all alone. Mara's demons surrounded the 'bo' tree.

Since Siddhattha sat there like a rock, Mara told his legions to attack from behind. Siddhattha saw that the gods had fled away and that there was no external aid of any kind. While the demons advanced he meditated steadfastly on the 'ten perfections' which he had all this time been cultivating as a bodhisatta. These would now be his only resource. Mara tried no less than nine fearsome elemental weapons. A whirlwind rushed up which would have ruined any of the towns round about, but it faded away just as it blew up to where Siddhattha sat. Torrential rain came next, soaking the forest to its roots, but somehow not a drop touched the vigilant's robe. Storms of flying rocks, flaming spears and burning coals came through the sky but dropped as flowers before his feet. Ashes, sand and mud came over in great clouds, but turned into fragrant sandal-wood, more flowers and perfumes. Lastly Mara conjured up a deep black darkness and then multiplied its degree of darkness by four, thus creating a terrifying threat to all sense of space and time. But in front of the Buddha-to-be it was dispersed as if by a bright sun.

Since all these onslaughts failed, Mara decided on a face-to-face confrontation. Mounted on his gigantic elephant he stood before the Buddha-to-be and demanded his seat. The latter listened and then declared steadily that Mara had not practised the ten perfections, nor renounced the world, nor sought after true knowledge and insight. The seat did not belong to Mara, but to himself, Siddhattha. Mara was beside himself with rage and hurled the emblem of his power, a spear-shaped javelin sharp enough to split a solid rock. It turned into a wonderful garland of flowers above Siddhattha's head. Ever more missiles flew and the devas gave him up for lost. But as they all turned into flowers at his feet the Buddha-to-be took the final initiative. Who, he asked, was Mara's witness that he had ever done any meritorious deed? At this Mara called upon all his evil companions to assert his merits, which they all resoundingly did. There was no one present on the other side it seemed, and Mara fell into the trap. Who indeed would witness for Siddhattha, he demanded. The latter drew out his right hand, pointed it downwards and required that the earth itself should witness to his many acts of merit in previous lives. The resulting thunderous earthquake was so tremendous that Mara's elephant knelt down in homage and all the demons fled in utter confusion.

Mara's daughters

With Mara's host dispersed the story continues on traditional lines. The sun set, and during the three watches of the night Gotama attained the 'three knowledges'. He meditated in direct and reverse order on the chain of Causal Arising (see earlier), and so attained complete enlightenment, his mind passing into nirvana. The mythological accompaniment to this event is quite dramatic.

Quite apart from a twelve-fold earthquake in ten thousand different worlds, everywhere was strewn with miraculous flowers of all kinds. The waters of the sea became sweet, the blind could see, the deaf could hear, and the lame could walk. These events are parallel to those which accompanied his birth.

While he sat on the seat of enlightenment he reflected that it was for this that he had gone through the trials and sacrifices of many previous existences. He would therefore sit there a little longer, and there he remained for seven days. Some of the devas watching over him grew concerned, thinking there might be something more which he had yet to achieve, but the Buddha calmed their fears by a miracle of bi-location. Rising into the air, he manifested himself simultaneously where he had been seated. This feat was sufficient to assuage the doubts of the devas.

Then he spent seven days standing a little further off and looking back at the seat where he had sat, another seven days walking back and forth along a bejewelled walk between the two spots, and yet another seven days in a shelter made of precious stones by the devas. All these elaborations serve to highlight the very spot where enlightenment was attained, a key reference point in the new religion.

The Buddha's encounters under various other trees have been related earlier, but a well-known addition in the mythologisation of the story is the approach of the daughters of Mara. The demon-king was defeated in principle, and we find him again sitting down in the road, more or less licking his wounds. All his efforts to find a chink in the Buddha's spiritual armour had failed. Moreover he disconsolately reviewed the positive qualities which the Buddha had cultivated, 'ten perfections' of giving, self-sacrifice, and so on, but which he himself had not developed. For each item of Buddhist virtue he doodled a line in the sand. Just then he was approached by his three daughters, Craving, Discontent and Lust personified. They found him looking downcast and asked the reason, which Mara explained. He was sure that nothing more could be done against so unwavering an adversary. The women however thought otherwise. Might they not yet distract him by their smooth words and sensual enticements? Off they went to find the Buddha, blatantly offering their services to gratify him. But he took not the slightest notice. The women reconsidered, for they knew their business. Different men have different tastes. Some prefer virgins and others prefer young women with some slight experience. Other men fall in love with more mature women, or with older women. Each of the three showed herself in a hundred magically enticing forms, and again and again they went up to the Buddha and flaunted themselves in bold or subtle ways. Finally the Buddha declared that they were wasting their time, for he was free from the craving, the discontent and the lust for which they stood. They had to admit defeat. Mara was overcome in principle and in practice.

16

A Buddha Walks the Earth

The Buddha proclaims Dhamma

Once Siddhattha had attained enlightenment and defeated the demon Mara, the story follows the pattern of the oldest tradition, which has already been given above. The newly enlightened Buddha was persuaded to proclaim his teaching by the god Brahma. He thought first of his two former teachers, Alara and Uddaka, but they had died. He travelled therefore to Benares, meeting the sceptical Upaka on the way (though the incident tends to be played down), and gave his teaching to the five ascetics who had been his companions before. Other conversions followed, as recounted earlier. His progress was accompanied by thousands of attendant devas. After he had been visited by King Bimbisara of Rajagaha, his suddenly increased popularity was such that he could hardly move along the roads. The god Sakka realised that his help was needed, because his throne began to feel hot, and therefore manifested himself as a particularly handsome young Brahman who led the way while uttering verses in the Buddha's praise.

The 'cosmological' impact of the appearance of a new Buddha is made abundantly clear. When King Bimbisara presented the Buddha with a place called the Bamboo Grove for a retreat there was an earthquake. This gift was a symbol of the founding of Buddhism, for it reflected both royal patronage and the existence of a semi-settled monastic community. But it was also a cosmic event, so to speak. This is supposed to have been the only *vihara* (monastery) in India, the acceptance of which as a gift, creating great merit, caused the earth to shake.

Another famous gift which found a permanent niche in the

story was the Jetavana Grove, presented by a wealthy householder named Anatha Pindika. The Jetavana Grove was a prize piece of land bought for a great sum by covering it with gold pieces, and was to be the crowning jewel in a whole chain of resting places for monks along the road between Rajagaha and Savatthi. At this choice spot was built a fine residence with many cells for monks which was dedicated with great pomp and ceremony. The Buddha is presented as explaining that a fixed residence protects the monks from cold and heat, as well as from animals and insects and of course above all from the weather during the rainy season. But this story is not just a rationalised recollection of the founding of a monastic settlement. The position of the Jetavana Grove is presumed to have been the very same spot where six previous Buddhas had had a monastery presented to them in very similar circumstances. Each time a wealthy merchant had bought the spot by covering it all over with gold, in the form of golden bricks, golden plough shares, golden elephants' feet or golden tortoises. It was another case of the cosmic repetition of the pattern of a Buddha's life.

The elaborated narratives still give surprisingly little detail of the Buddha's life as a wandering and authoritative teacher. The *Nidanakatha* ends with the founding of the Jetavana Vihara, while the *Mahavastu*, though prolific in additional stories about the past, only takes us through to the conversion of King Bimbisara. It is not until the commentary on the *Buddhavamsa* that we have a list of places where the Buddha stayed over a period of twenty years, but this provides nothing more than an artificial thread for some of the more secondary anecdotes scattered about various other texts. There are, however, a few other sequences which became well-known parts of the Buddha's life story. These probably arose to meet a need for more personalised drama in the recollection of the Buddha's life.

While the Buddha was staying in the Bamboo Grove near Rajagaha his fame reached his father, King Suddhodana in Kapilavatthu. The son who had left home six years before was now a Buddha proclaiming Dhamma. As soon as he heard the news he sent off a courtier with a retinue of 1,000 men, with instructions to request the Buddha to return and see his father. When they arrived they heard the Buddha teaching his doctrine, were converted, immediately ordained, and presented with miraculously created robes and bowls. On being converted they achieved the highest spiritual condition for a Buddhist disciple, arahantship, and for this reason lost all interest in worldly matters. The message was therefore never conveyed. Other messengers were sent, and altogether no less than 9,000 men were converted in this way.

Finally the king sent a most trusted friend named Kala Udayin, who had once been a playmate of the Buddha as a child. This man promised to deliver the message if he might have permission to become a monk first. When this was granted he went off and got converted like the others. After the rainy season and the winter had passed, Udayin began to praise the pleasures of travelling in spring-time. When the Buddha asked him the reason for his enthusiasm, he gave his message, and the Buddha agreed to return to Kapilavatthu. He was accompanied by the 10,000 monks who had come from Kapilavatthu, and another 10,000 from the area around Magadha. The journey took two months. Udayin had attained supernormal powers and could fly through the air. He went on ahead and told King Suddhodana of the Buddha's progress. Then he returned each day, by magical flight, with a bowl of food presented by the king to his son. Meanwhile the Sakya people prepared for the Buddha to stay at a place called the Nigrodha Grove.

Here the Buddha's former compatriots and kinsmen came to have audience with him, but only the children were made to show reverence. The others just sat down by virtue of their seniority of age. At this the Buddha promptly threw a miracle, preaching his doctrine by walking up and down in the sky. The king recalled those occasions in the Buddha's infancy when he had himself paid obeisance. Now he did so again, and all the other Sakyas followed suit.

Then came a mighty shower of rain. This too was a miracle, for anybody who wished to get wet did so, and anybody who did not want to get wet remained dry. So they all listened to his teaching with respect.

Since nobody asked him to eat with them the next day the Buddha went on his begging rounds from house to house. He was seen from a window by Yasodhara, his wife of years before. She was transfixed by his appearance for he displayed the thirty-two marks of a 'great man' and illuminated the whole street with a radiant halo. She reported it to the king who was deeply shocked that a Sakya should beg for food. The Buddha declared that in the succession of the Buddhas, to which he belonged, all had begged for their food. The king, who was by now an ailing man, heard his son proclaim his teaching from the street. From this point onwards it began to have a strong attraction for him; and eventually he was to attain arahantship without ever leaving home, on his death-bed.

In the meantime food was served in the palace, and only Yasodhara did not attend. She was waiting for the Buddha to take the initiative in visiting her, which he did, with his two chief monks, Moggallana and Sariputta. She then paid obeisance to him as a Buddha, and he heard how she had followed his own customs in his absence, clothing herself in yellow, taking but one meal a day, sleeping on the floor instead of on a raised bed, and giving up the use of flowers and cosmetics. The story of how she sent their son Rahula to claim his 'inheritance' from the Buddha has been told before, because it appears prominently in the books of discipline. The request led to Rahula's ordination, and to the ruling that parents' permission was necessary before a son could be ordained.

Others ordained at Kapilavatthu are said to have included Ananda and Anuruddha, two monks prominent in the story of the Buddha's last days. Ananda is supposed to have become the Buddha's personal attendant some twenty years after the enlightenment. Another prominent convert was Nanda, a stepbrother of the Buddha himself. He was about to be married but left his bride, to her great chagrin, in order to take the Buddha's begging bowl back to the Nigrodha Grove. The Buddha had 'forgotten' it on purpose, to draw Nanda in. Once there he found himself ordained in a jiffy, more or less out of politeness. This is the same Nanda who is supposed later to have hankered after his wife until the Buddha miraculously showed him beautiful celestial women, among whom he might hope to be reborn. He stayed in the order for this reason, but eventually progressed beyond desire for women.

It is related that years afterwards Nanda's mother, named Mahapajapati, sought ordination. She had been indeed the

Buddha's own stepmother who fostered him as a child. At first he would not listen, refusing the request through Ananda three times. Mahapajapati however followed after the Buddha, with other women, all wearing yellow robes. Again they were refused. Finally Ananda asked whether women could attain the four 'fruits' of spiritual life (stream-winner, once-returner, never-returner and arahant), and on hearing that they could, he pleaded with the Buddha to accept this woman, who had fed him at her own breast. The Buddha relented and allowed ordination of nuns, on the basis of special rules which emphasised the dominant role of monks. The existence of an order of nuns from an early date is surely historical, because of the existence of rules for nuns and also the regular way of describing the Buddha's disciples as monks and nuns, laymen and laywomen. However there seems little doubt that in spite of the loyalty and sanctity of the various women about whom stories are told, the Buddha saw women as being a dangerous obstacle in the path to enlightenment.

The story of the Buddha's early visit to Kapilavatthu stresses his powers as a miracle worker, but more importantly it emphasises his chosen destiny as a Buddha rather than as a king. The conflict of interest with his father which had led to a dramatic rejection of home or palace life was resolved by the eventual conversion of not only his father but also other relatives and notables. It is even held that he sojourned in the heavens to convert his mother. However, this acquiescence was not permanent in the mind of one convert, namely his cousin Devadatta.

Devadatta is mentioned sometimes just as one monk among others; although the foreknowledge of the story-tellers led to anecdotes of more youthful rivalry, as in the case of the slaying of the white elephant mentioned earlier. Devadatta features above all however as a rival holy man, himself already gifted with miraculous powers, which rapidly waned as his thoughts turned to evil. He nursed an ambition to direct and control others, thought that he might displace the Buddha himself, and when the latter in fairly advanced age refused to make him successor, he took to politicking to gain his ends. The story is that he teamed up with Ajatasattu, the ruthless son of King Bimbisara. Each was to slay the present holder of political and religious authority respectively.

Each would then rule instead. Ajatasattu did kill his own father Bimbisara, and thereby seized the throne of Magadha. Devadatta's schemes to kill the Buddha were all miraculously thwarted. When he crashed a rock down the mountainside at him, it split in two, one half rolling past the Buddha on each side. But the most notorious attempt to take the Buddha's life, often depicted in illustrations, was with a rogue elephant. This beast was let loose on the highway, drunken and fierce. It rushed through the streets of Rajagaha, killing many and scattering the rest. The Buddha was just entering the town and received many warnings from onlookers on gates and in buildings. His attendant company of monks all fled away, except for Ananda. Guardian devas thronged the skies, but above all the Buddha himself was composed and steadfast in himself as the maddened animal came at him. When the elephant saw this calm unmoving figure, he also stopped, and then fell on his knees to the ground. The Buddha spoke to him. Elephants too are driven astray by the 'cankers' of lust, anger and delusion, and therefore are reborn unhappily, but elephants too can give them up and find peace. The elephant was converted, and the people watching cheered and brought offerings. Even Ajatasattu was moved by new thoughts of self-examination and virtue. Devadatta's plans of dominion were by now quite hopeless, and although he had once attained a high level of spiritual powers his misdeeds brought him age-long sufferings in the lowest hell.

The Parinirvana

One might begin again at this point with the opening of the great sutra on the Buddha's nirvana, with Ajatasattu seeking the Buddha's advice on warlike projects. This would lead us in to the cycle of legends treated before as one of the fundamental growing points of narrative about the Buddha. The reader may recall the anecdote about the Buddha inspecting fortifications at Pataligama, on the Magadha side of the Ganges. A Chinese version of the *Buddhacarita* in fact takes up this story immediately after the chapter on Devadatta, and leads in from there into the story of the Buddha's nirvana. In such ways a biography of sorts was stitched together in the minds of Buddhists in later centuries.

However this completed story was by no means biography in a modern sense. It was simply a narrative extension of the mythological life-pattern of each and every Buddha. The mythological frame-work provided a home for smaller points of personal detail or reminiscence which themselves had grown considerably in the telling.

The story of the Buddha's last days was already mythologised in the form in which we have it, whether we look at the Pali transmission, or indeed at the Sanskrit one which Waldschmidt argued to be on balance more archaic. One has only to recall the causes of an earthquake: leaving the heavens, birth, enlightenment and first teaching. These are followed by another earthquake when the Buddha decides not to prolong his life, and another when he passes away. The food which leads to a Buddha's death is one of the most meritorious of all offerings. The devas weep at the thought of his death, or are unshaken in mind, just as the humans. The devas also control the transportation of the Buddha's body, for the eight Malla chiefs who tried to do so simply could not lift it when they were intending to take it in the wrong direction. Through the whole story there is a sense of predetermined direction, which fits after all with the Buddha-to-be deciding to be born, where to be born, when to be born, and so on. Throughout his life the mythologised Buddha moves unchecked, escorted by the devas to his Enlightenment and eventually to his nirvana. When the Buddha passed away, the praise of nirvana was sung out by two devas suspended in the heavens. Then followed the human Anuruddha. But whether the voice was human or celestial the message was the same, namely praise for the Buddha's achievement.

Illustrations of the Buddha's attainment of nirvana (*parinibbana*) show him lying in the position described before, between the hospitable sal trees, with many looking on and mourning, while others were self-composed. It was understood to be a very special death, nirvana 'without remainder', that is, leaving no residue of karmic forces which would pass on to seek outlet in yet another human life of suffering. It was presumed to be not some blissful sojourn in long-lasting heavens, nor on the other hand a destructive annihilation or nihilism, but a mysterious liberation from the conditions which lead again and again to suffering. All that was left of him in the world of the senses were his funeral relics, karmically inactive as far as the Buddha himself was concerned, but immensely potent in the devotional life of his followers.

A Twentieth-Century Postscript

Buddhism has seen some remarkable modern revivals in traditionally Buddhist countries. In Burma, Thailand, Ceylon and Vietnam it has been of particular importance as an element in the national self-consciousness. Its destiny in present-day China is largely a matter of speculation, as far as outsiders are concerned, but Buddhism in its Mahayana ('great vehicle') form continues to flourish in other East Asian countries. At the same time the modern world moves at a tempo quite unknown to the Buddha and his first followers. Just as the people's revolution in China has left Buddhism on one side, so too has the irresistable power of industry and commerce in Japan. Buddhism has been shunted on to a few neglected sidings. There are some well-tended historic survivals and a residual rural Buddhism, there are family connections remembered on the occasion of funerals, and there are cults catering for the needs of individuals uprooted by rapid social change. But the total picture of Buddhism in Asia is extremely complex. How could it be otherwise when one refers to more than one thousand million people in widely differing stages of political, economic and cultural development!

However we might chart the persistence or the demise of Buddhist social patterns in Asia, Buddhism is undeniably one of the major constituents of the cultural memory of mankind as a whole. Its adoption as a personal religion by a few western enthusiasts is relatively trivial by comparison with this wider cultural claim. The reader might quite fairly ask what Buddhism means or could mean for the western world of Europe and America. But from a truly intercultural standpoint the question is really about the meaning of Buddhism for the whole modern world. The modern world in general has a wider cultural memory than that of Europe or America alone. It is a memory in which all significant traditions are shared. In this sense Buddhism belongs to us all, as indeed do Christianity, the great movements of intellectual and social liberation in modern history, and so on.

If the chosen path of the Buddha himself was a challenge to the society of his day, so it is to that of the modern world. His life-story dramatises a rejection of wealth, power and pleasure-seeking. Grasping after these leads only to suffering, eventually if not immediately. Thus the reason for detachment is not some mere condemnation of enjoyment for its own sake, but a search for a deeper and lasting state of well-being. Tortuous self-denial was also abandoned by the Buddha, for it would simply be a kind of spiritual grasping. His aim might be defined as moving lightly through the world, accepting the necessities of life as they come, but not acting in any way which would fuel the process of suffering for himself or others.

The pure model of Buddhist life is that of the homeless wanderer, renouncing the household life, taking no part in worldly activities, living on offerings made by others. How would it be if such a model were universally followed? World financial centres such as London, Tokyo and New York would collapse. Other economic and political capitals such as Moscow, Brussels and Peking, would be sapped of their strength. The world as we know it would fall into ruins. But the Buddha was a pragmatist with a long-term perspective. His mode of life, and that of his followers, was dependent on the good-will of a world which had not yet renounced itself. Not all young men are expected to become monks, though it seems enough did so long ago in Magadha to cause concern to respectable society.

It is also apparent that from early times a less dramatic form of Buddhism was acceptable, the Buddhism of the lay householder involved in domestic, social and political life. This ideal was carried forward with particular verve in the Mahayana Buddhism of East Asia, which saw many paradoxical transformations of the original simple message. Thus the discipline of non-attachment, non-grasping, non-aggression, found ways of influencing the style of life of merchants, warriors and politicians. Viewed cynically, one might think of this as an excuse for making money in a relaxed way. But though Buddhism undoubtedly has suffered real distortion at times, the overall perspective must be fairly viewed.

It really involves accepting the pragmatic necessity of worldly activity, as the context in which detachment from the causes of suffering can be learned. It is probably in the inward acceptance of such attitudes that the meaning of Buddhism is generally relevant to modern times, rather than in attempts to form a distinct worldwide monastic order, obtaining food and clothing on the basis of an archaic doctrine of merit.

In the story of the Buddha himself, renunciation meant not becoming king, abandoning harem and wife, etc. But apart from these practical and sensual matters, which some modern playboys and power-seekers might wish to emulate, there is also a mental aspect to renunciation. This means learning non-attachment to, for example, either nihilist or eternalist views of the world: both being speculative vices which betray a kind of spiritual bondage. It means recognising the practical necessity of conceptual systems, whether for politics, economics, morals or religion, while learning inwardly how to do without them. It means using mental constructs without coercion or self-imprisonment. This is a style which every Buddhist has to learn for himself (and not all succeed at once). But it is also a gift to the modern world in general, which suffers so much from the mental and social constructions of desire.

As for westerners, Buddhism will no doubt always have for us something of the exotic lure of the East. Many of the social patterns into which Buddhism was channelled over centuries have no relevance at all for Europe and America. To adopt some fastidiously imitated form of Buddhism would both be quite artificial and also would indicate immaturity with respect to our own social and religious roots. Yet it is very worth while for westerners to sift and to search the Buddhist tradition of Asia. It bears insights which ought to contribute to the emerging global culture of modern times, a culture which is shared by all mankind.

Note on Sources

Any modern writer on Buddhism is in debt to the Pali Text Society, and the influence of T. W. Rhys Davids' translation of the *Digha Nikaya* as *Dialogues of the Buddha* (3 vols., with Mrs C. A. F. Rhys Davids, 1899–1921) and of Miss I. B. Horner's translation of the *Majjhima Nikaya* as *Middle Length Sayings* (3 vols, 1954–9) will be evident to those familiar with them. Miss Horner's translation of the *Book of the Discipline* (6 vols, 1938–66) was also indispensable, as indeed were various other volumes of the Pali Canon, to which reference is sometimes made. These translations published by the Pali Text Society have been accepted as authoritative, though a number of technical terms have been chased back into the Pali original. Another important piece by Rhys Davids was his translation of the *Nidana Katha* in *Buddhist Birth Stories* Vol. 1 (London 1880). This is similar to an archaic translation of the *Maduratthavilasini* by G. Turnour in the *Journal of the Bengal Asiatic Society* Vol. VII (Sept. 1838).

As to Sanskrit works, J. J. Jones' translation of *The Mahavastu* (3 vols. 1949–56) was published by the Pali Text Society; the *Buddhacarita* has had several versions made including E. B. Cowell in the *Sacred Books of the East* Vol. XLIX (1894), S. Beal from a Chinese version in the same series Vol. XIX (1883), and E. H. Johnston *The Buddhacarita, or Acts of the Buddha* (Lahore 1936); the main version of The *Lalitavistara* consulted was that of R. Mitra (Calcutta 1882).

It would lead too far to list all the books about Buddhism which have had some influence on my treatment. Suffice it to name three which were of importance. The first two are mentioned in Chapter 1. E. J. Thomas' *The Life of the Buddha* (London 1927, 3rd. ed. 1949), was a pioneer work, still concerned with shaking off the quasi-historical claims of The *Lalitavistara,* etc., but useful on many miscellaneous matters. E. Lamotte's *Histoire du Bouddhisme Indien* (Louvain 1958) was taken to be an authoritative general account of the early history of Buddhism. Above all acknowledgement must be made of the immense value of Ernst Waldschmidt's great researches into the nirvana narrative in *Die Überlieferung vom Lebensende des Buddha* (Göttingen 1944 and 1948). This important critical tool was not available to Thomas when he wrote his above-mentioned book; nor does it seem to have been used by other writers in English since. As far as Part Three of this book is concerned Waldschmidt's work has been consulted page by page. In addition, some use was made of Waldschmidt's parallel edition of the Sanskrit and Pali texts, with his accompanying translation of a Chinese version, entitled *Das Mahaparinirvanasutra* in *Abhandlungen der deutschen Akademie der Wissenschaften zu Berlin* Jahrgang 1950 Nos. 2 and 3 (Berlin 1951).

M.P.

Index